ELEMENTARY EDUCATOR'S GUIDE TO PRIMARY SOURCES

ELEMENTARY EDUCATOR'S GUIDE TO PRIMARY SOURCES

Strategies for Teaching

Tom Bober

LIBRARIES UNLIMITED™

An Imprint of ABC-CLIO, LLC

Santa Barbara, California • Denver, Colorado

Library of Congress Cataloging in Publication Control Number: 2018035842

ISBN: 978–1–4408–6386–8 (paperback)
      978–1–4408–6387–5 (eBook)

23 22 21 20 19   1 2 3 4 5

This book is also available as an eBook.

Libraries Unlimited
An Imprint of ABC-CLIO, LLC

ABC-CLIO, LLC
130 Cremona Drive, P.O. Box 1911
Santa Barbara, California 93116-1911
www.abc-clio.com

This book is printed on acid-free paper ∞

Manufactured in the United States of America

To my father for the excitement he had in everything that
I do and to my wife for her unquestioning support in it all.

Contents

Acknowledgments   xiii

CHAPTER 1:   An Introduction to Primary Sources   1
Analyzing Primary Sources as a Key Skill in Learning   2
What Is a Primary Source?   5
Where to Find Primary Sources   7
Preparing to Use Primary Sources and This Book   9

**CHAPTER 2:   Analyzing Primary Sources in the
                Elementary Grades**   13
What Happens in Every Primary-Source-Analysis Strategy   14
    A Teacher Frames the Primary Source Analysis   14
    Students Work within the Framework to Analyze the
    Primary Source   15
    Students Collaborate through the Analysis   16
    Primary Source Analysis Connects to Other Learning   17
Strategy 1: See, Think, Wonder Strategy   17
    Strategy Overview   17
    Framing the See, Think, Wonder Strategy for Students   18
    Guiding Students through the See, Think, Wonder Strategy   20
        Guiding Students in Seeing the Primary Source   20
        Guiding Students in Thinking about the Primary Source   22
        Guiding Students in Wondering about a Primary Source   23
    Teacher's Role in the See, Think, Wonder Strategy   25
        Teacher Roles Often Taken On   25

Teacher Roles to Avoid Taking On   26
Teacher Roles Sometimes Taken On   27
Differentiating the See, Think, Wonder Strategy
for Youngest Learners   29
Strategy 2: Close Reading Strategy   30
Strategy Overview   31
Framing the Close Reading Strategy for Students   31
Guiding Students through the Close Reading Strategy   33
Guiding Students to Read through a Lens   33
Guiding Students through Finding Patterns   35
Guiding Students through Developing Understanding   37
Teacher's Role in the Close Reading Strategy   39
Teacher Roles Often Taken On   39
Teacher Roles to Avoid Taking On   40
Teacher Roles Sometimes Taken On   41
Differentiating the Close Reading Strategy for Youngest Learners   42
Strategy 3: See, Wonder, Think Strategy   43
Strategy Overview   43
Framing the See, Wonder, Think Strategy for Students   43
Guiding Students through the See, Wonder, Think Strategy   46
Guiding Students in Seeing the Primary Source   47
Guiding Students in Wondering about the Primary Source   48
Guiding Students in Thinking about the Primary Source   50
Teacher's Role in the See, Wonder, Think Strategy   53
Teacher Roles Often Taken On   53
Teacher Roles to Avoid Taking On   54
Teacher Roles Sometimes Taken On   55
Differentiating the See, Wonder, Think Strategy for
Youngest Learners   56
Strategy 4: Analyzing Like a Historian Strategy   57
Strategy Overview   57
Framing the Analyzing Like a Historian Strategy for Students   57
Guiding Students through the Analyzing Like a Historian Strategy   59
Guiding Students through Sourcing   60
Guiding Students through Contextualization   62
Guiding Students through Analyzing the Source   63
Guiding Students through Corroboration   65
Teacher's Role in the Analyzing Like a Historian Strategy   66
Teacher Roles Often Taken On   66
Teacher Roles to Avoid Taking On   67
Teacher Roles Sometimes Taken On   69

Differentiating the Analyzing Like a Historian
Strategy for Youngest Learners   70
A Special Note about the Analyzing Like a
Historian Strategy   70
Strategy 5: Using Visible Thinking Strategies as Exit Slips   71
   Strategies Overview   71
   Framing the Visible Thinking Strategies for Students   72
   Guiding Students through Visible Thinking Strategies   72
   Examples of Exit Slips in Use   73
   Teacher's Role in Visible Thinking Strategies   76
     Teacher Roles Often Taken On   76
     Teacher Roles to Avoid Taking On   77
     Teacher Roles Sometimes Taken On   77
   Differentiating Visible Thinking Strategies for
   Youngest Learners   78

CHAPTER 3: Selecting Primary Sources   79
Choosing Compelling Primary Sources   80
   What Makes a Primary Source Compelling?   81
     Connection   81
     Well-Known or Familiar   81
     Makes You Wonder   82
     Format   82
     Elicits an Emotion   82
Analyzing Primary Source Images   85
   Types of Primary Source Images   85
   Considerations When Selecting Primary Source Images   85
     Portraits, Drawings, Sketches, and Engravings   85
     Text in Primary Source Images   86
   Student Interactions with Primary Source Images   87
     Determining How Students Will Interact with the Source   87
     Modified Analysis for Primary Source Images   89
       Puzzle Strategy   90
       Jump In Strategy   92
       Pose Strategy   93
Analyzing Primary Source Text   95
   Types of Primary Source Texts   95
   Considerations When Selecting Primary Source Texts   96
     Challenging Vocabulary in Primary Source Texts   96
     Handwriting in Primary Source Texts   97
     The Long S in Primary Source Texts   99

Long Passages of Primary Source Text 100
Images in Primary Source Text 101
Student Interactions with Primary Source Texts 101
Determining How Students Will Interact with the Source 101
Transcripts of Primary Source Text 103
Jigsaw Strategy 103
Writing a Headline to Summarize 104
Analyzing Primary Source Sounds and Moving Pictures 105
Types of Primary Source Sounds and Moving Pictures 105
Considerations When Selecting Primary Source
Sounds and Moving Pictures 106
Time Available to Interact with the Source 106
Supporting Sound of the Primary Source 106
Movement within the Primary Source 107
Emotion Shown through the Primary Source 107
Equipment Needed to Interact with Audiovisual
Primary Sources 109
Student Interactions with Primary Source Sounds and
Moving Pictures 109
Active versus Passive Use 109
Student Control of Access to the Primary Source 110
Documenting Primary Source Audio Analysis 110
Documenting Primary Source Video and Film Analysis 112

CHAPTER 4: Connecting Primary Sources to
Content Curriculum 113
Viewing Primary Sources through a Subject Area Lens 114
Primary Sources and Social Studies 116
Primary Sources and Language Arts 121
Primary Sources and Science 128
Primary Sources and Math 130

CHAPTER 5: Assuring Success with Primary Source Analysis:
Teacher Tips 133
Collaborative Classroom Culture during Primary Source Analysis 134
Collaboration Configurations during Primary Source Analysis 134
Whole-Class Collaboration 134
Small-Group Collaboration 134
Pair Collaboration 135
Mixing Collaborations during Primary Source Analysis 136
Collaboration as a Way to Address Student Misconceptions 137

Considering Moment of Use	139
Primary Sources at the Beginning of a Lesson	139
Primary Sources as Part of Whole-Class Instruction	140
Primary Sources during Independent Instruction	141
Primary Sources Analysis as Assessment	143
Listening and Responding during Primary Source Analysis	145
Listening during a Primary Source Analysis	145
Responding during a Primary Source Analysis	148
Pairing Primary Sources for Student Learning	151
Why Pair Primary Sources?	151
Pairing Primary Sources with Multiple Perspectives	151
Pairing Primary Sources to Fill in the Gaps or Answer Questions	152
Pairing Primary Sources to Reinforce Understandings and Ideas	154
Pairing Primary Sources to Extend or Broaden a Topic	155
An Additional Note on Analyzing Paired Primary Sources	157
A Final Hope and Setting Goals to Use Primary Source Analysis with Elementary Students	157
Bibliography	159
Primary Source References	161
Index	165

Acknowledgments

As finishing touches are put on this book, I can look back at one pivotal moment in the journey. I had just started to see great learning coming from using primary sources. After telling stories to a Meg Steele, who was working at the Library of Congress, and swiping through pictures of students' work on my phone, her response was, "You need to think about sharing this with people!" That day I made a decision to start sharing beyond my library. That journey of speaking, writing, and working with amazing educators has also had many supporters along the way.

Many thanks go to the rest of the Educational Outreach staff at the Library of Congress who welcomed me for a year as a Teacher in Residence and encouraged my ideas as well as my growth. Special thanks to Cheryl Lederle, my unofficial mentor during my time there, and Lee Ann Potter, who believed I had something to offer and brought me in for the most amazing year of professional growth I've ever experienced. Thanks also to Mary Johnson and the Teaching with Primary Sources Teachers Network Mentors. You give me a supported place to continue that growth that I appreciate every day.

My appreciation also goes to my administration in my school and district as well as my classroom teachers. When I want to try something new, something I am unsure will work, you have the opportunity to tell me no and yet continue to say yes. I hope it is the student growth and engaged learning that keep you letting me take risks and see awesome rewards. A special thanks to Sean Doherty, my former principal and current superintendent, who sees the benefit my professional growth has on student learning, and to Jennifer Martin, my principal, who appreciates the gains that my reaching out and working with educators outside of the district have on my own growth as well as student learning in the school.

Much gratitude is also shared with ABC-CLIO and Classroom Library Connection, who saw value in this work and me. Special thanks to Paige Jaeger, who saw me speak at a conference and thought I had an article in me; David Paige, who read my articles and thought I might have a book in me; and Sharon Coatney, my editor for this work.

Lastly, my eternal thanks go to my family, who regularly sacrifices time for me to do this positive work. I love being able to share good news and celebrate small moments with you. My greatest thanks go to my wife, Jen. Not only did you inspire me to become a school librarian but you also have supported me in every way through every step of this journey. I cannot thank you enough.

Chapter 1

An Introduction to Primary Sources

I love old documents. I always have. Older letters, photos, drawings, maps, and films have always fascinated me. I get lost in them, putting myself in the moment, looking for details that place them uniquely in time, comparing aspects of them to today, and wondering about the people or moment in the source.

That excitement was probably why years ago, when I came across digitized historical resources from the Library of Congress, I couldn't wait to bring them to my fifth-grade students. I soon ran into a problem. I had no idea how to help students interact with these types of sources. As much as I hoped my students would be as enamored with the documents as I was, that didn't happen. Instead, the lesson fell flat, my students were disinterested, and I became disenchanted with using these resources with my students.

Sometime later, I was able to attend an institute that opened my eyes. What I was missing were strategies for my students to use to analyze primary sources. I left the best professional development of my life, ready to redeem myself and excited to bring these artifacts to my students. At this point, I was in the library of my elementary school and had the opportunity to begin using resources with students from kindergarten through fifth grade.

The results were better than I expected. As my students began interacting with primary sources, the first thing I noticed was the engagement. Students who often stayed in the background were offering their voices to discussions in the library. Others who were easily distracted were drawn into the learning more than I had seen before. The second benefit that I saw was the deep levels of thinking my students demonstrated. Connections to other learning and their own lives played a role as students made meaning from these historical artifacts. Thought-provoking questions that I would not have anticipated were posed by my youngest students. Lastly, students collaborated in ways that were new to me. Not only did they work together but they also listened to each other and built upon each other's ideas.

But those results didn't happen the first time my students used primary sources or even the second. Instead, the benefits slowly revealed themselves. Over time, I came to realize that part of the reason was that it took them time to learn how to interact with primary sources and each other in new ways. The

Students collaborated in ways that were new to me.

other part was slower to show itself, but I soon realized that these amazing benefits in my students' learning also took time because I was learning to teach in a new way. One week at the institute gave me tools, but it took me time to learn to use them.

This book is meant to give you tools, or frameworks, that I find invaluable when using primary sources as a part of student learning. It also focuses on special considerations when using these frameworks with young learners. There will be learning involved, for you and for your students, but my hope is that you will reflect on the suggestions in this book as well as your own teaching as you and your students become experts in teaching with and making meaning from primary sources.

Analyzing Primary Sources as a Key Skill in Learning

There are a number of skills that go into analyzing primary sources. Visual literacy will be used when analyzing a historical photo. Foundational literacy plays a role when reading a diary account. Even media literacy is needed to carefully examine old advertisements. Students will collaborate when working together, evaluate when discovering and deciding upon their own found sources, or construct meaning as they identify and interpret aspects of a map.

While planning to analyze primary sources and the learning that happens with that analysis, we can also look to school, district, and national goals and standards to see where connections can be made. Whether you look to the National Council for the Social Studies (NCSS) College, Career, and Civic Life (C3) Framework, the Next Generation Science Standards, American Association of School Librarians (AASL) National School Library Standards, or other national standards, these skills and others are highlighted as important to student learning. Later, we will look at four critical skills that are developed through work elementary students can do with primary sources and that are also expressed in many sets of standards and goals. We will also use competencies in the National School Library Standards: AASL Standards Framework for Learners to highlight the connection between standards and learning with primary sources in the elementary classroom.

There are standards that speak to student inquiry, encouraging students to develop their own questions as well as plan and implement how to answer them. Primary sources can be used to both inspire student questions and uncover information to answer those questions. Looking specifically at the National School Library Standards: AASL Standards Framework for Learners, ideas around inquiry can be seen through competencies under the shared foundations of Inquiring and Exploring.

Inquiring:

- Using evidence to investigate questions
- Enacting new understanding through real-world connections

Exploring:

- Reflecting and questioning assumptions and possible misconceptions
- Expressing curiosity about a topic of personal interest or curricular relevance

Other standards describe the need for students to seek out and identify perspectives and points of view. Primary sources share a moment in history through the perspective of the person who created the document. Elementary students can begin to identify those perspectives and think about how they shape what they are seeing in the primary source. The importance of exploring perspectives is highlighted in the National School Library Standards: AASL Standards Framework for Learners under the shared foundation of Including.

Including:

- Adopting a discerning stance toward points of view and opinions expressed in information resources and learning products
- Evaluating a variety of perspectives during learning activities

That point of view is not always apparent to the student but can be discovered through the analysis process. The analysis of primary sources connects with other standards in these documents that speak to evaluating sources. The primary-source-analysis processes in this book allow students to evaluate a variety of different formats of primary sources from images to text to audiovisual. The importance of analysis and evaluating can be seen in the National School Library Standards: AASL Standards Framework for Learners under the shared foundations of Curating and Engaging.

Curating:

- Making critical choices about information sources to use
- Openly communicating curation processes for others to use, interpret, and validate

Engaging:

- Evaluating information for accuracy, validity, social and cultural context, and appropriateness for need
- Acknowledging authorship and demonstrating respect for the intellectual property of others

Finally, national standards often promote students interacting with the real world. Primary sources, whether they were created yesterday or centuries ago, connect students to that real world that we want them to interact with. Students connect with a person, event, moment, or place through primary sources that shape their understanding of the past and the present. Elementary students also connect with each other when analyzing a primary source, making their learning a shared event. This skill of shared learning and connecting with others is evident in the National School Library Standards: AASL Standards Framework for Learners when viewing the shared foundation of Collaborating.

Collaborating:

- Developing new understandings through engagement in a learning group
- Actively contributing to group discussions

There may be similar standards or goals in state, district, or school documents you are tasked with addressing in your students' learning. Even if some of the aforementioned standards are not similar to the ones that you explicitly address, you would probably agree that these are important skills for elementary students to be working toward. The analysis of primary sources not only builds these skill sets but also, as you will read in Chapter 4, has the strongest benefit when connected with content that is already taught in your classroom.

What Is a Primary Source?

Before delving too deeply into how primary sources can be used with elementary students, we should define a primary source. There are many definitions for primary sources. They can be found on the websites of institutions that share historical documents, in textbooks, and in our own minds.

For the purposes of this book and the examples within it, I would like to share my own working definition: *A primary source is an item directly connected to a topic and related time.* If students were, for example, studying the building of the Statue of Liberty, a primary source would be any item connected to the Statue of Liberty and the time when it was being built. That might include architectural plans, photographs or drawings of the statue, or newspaper articles about the

Students studying the building of the Statue of Liberty viewing a primary source.

building of the statue from that time period. Resources about the Statue of Liberty created outside of the years when it was being planned and built would, in this case, be considered secondary sources for our topic of study. Expository nonfiction about the statue would be an obvious example of a secondary source, but other examples might include online writings, photographs, videos, radio programming, or news articles about the statue created after it was built.

Speaking to many educators and students over the years, I found there are some common misconceptions around defining a primary source. Some of these misconceptions are supported by the definitions shared through trusted institutions. Others are reinforced by how teachers and students have traditionally incorporated different types of sources into student learning.

A first common misconception is that a source is always primary or secondary. In fact, a source is primary, secondary, or not a source at all on the basis of the topic being studied. In our previous example, a letter written by George Washington would have nothing to do with the building of the Statue of Liberty and would not be a source for our study of that topic. I have seen many definitions of primary sources, though, that contain examples of formats such as letters or photos to explain what a primary source is. There is also a classic activity where elementary students show their understanding of primary sources by sorting items into two categories: primary and secondary. Students are told they are correct when they sort items such as letters, diaries, and photographs into the primary source pile and other items such as books, encyclopedias, and websites into the secondary source pile. This activity reinforces this misconception that any item of a particular format is always a primary source. We can see, though, that this isn't the case.

A second misconception is that primary sources are "true" or "factual," while secondary sources are "biased" or "someone's opinion." When this concept is conveyed by a teacher, students are left with the idea that primary sources are better than secondary sources. Teachers and students will find, when analyzing a primary source, that it is riddled with perspective and bias from the individual who created the source. In fact, the perspective and bias evident in the primary source is often what makes the source interesting to interact with and learn from. In addition, there are many benefits from using secondary sources, both on their own and in connection with primary sources. To value one over the other ignores the possibility that a secondary source may help a student understand the confusing elements of a primary source or that a primary source can add depth to the understanding a student gains from a secondary source.

A final misconception that teachers often convey is that a primary source is created by an individual with a firsthand account of the event. While this is the most widespread of the misconceptions, there are two reasons teachers should stop teaching this as a measuring device when determining whether a source is primary or secondary.

The first reason is that while the definitions of a primary source often contain the idea of it being a firsthand account, in practice, this is typically not used. One example is the engraving by Paul Revere of the Boston Massacre. This print is regularly referred to as a primary source of the event, but Revere was not on King Street on March 5, 1770. His work, though coming out three weeks after the event, shaped public perception of the event and should be used today as a primary source when studying the Boston Massacre and its impact. Look at lists of documents described as primary sources on the websites of trusted institutions. It becomes evident that many of these sources are not firsthand accounts but are instead connected to the topic under study and from the time period. This may include immediate reaction to the event in letters, newspapers, or artistic interpretations such as Revere's engraving.

The second reason not to focus on firsthand accounts is that they can be very difficult to verify. Historic items often are identified by a date or date range when they are believed to have been created. There may also be a person attributed with creating the item. Determining whether that person was at the event itself can be challenging or impossible with some formats like manuscripts, newspaper articles, or maps. Not only will this extra criterion frustrate teachers when identifying primary sources to use with students but it will also confuse students when they begin searching for their own primary sources, possibly causing them to abandon sources that could lead to valuable learning. Instead, the definition should assist teachers and students in identifying the item as primary or secondary, not confuse them, making them feel as if they are somehow not able to grasp the finer points of identifying a primary source. Instead, use a straightforward definition. If the item is connected to the topic of study and the time period, label it as a primary source and move to the important work of analysis.

Where to Find Primary Sources

This book does not explore every possible place, online and in person, for identifying primary sources. Nor does it delve into the nuances of search strategies to find these sources. Finding the sources, though, is an important aspect of bringing them to your students. The following are several starting points I use when I am searching for primary sources for elementary lessons. This list is by no means exhaustive. You may already have favorite sites or other resources to access primary sources. The important point is not where you find primary sources for your elementary students to use but that your students have the opportunity to use them.

Library of Congress (loc.gov): This treasure trove of sources has millions of digitized items available. The strength of their collection is in items from the United States prior to 1922, but they have many collections of sources beyond this date.

A variety of different formats can be found by searching from the main page, but Primary Source Sets can also be found on their Teachers page (loc.gov/teachers). Use these sets as they are or as inspiration for related searches.

Chronicling America (chroniclingamerica.loc.gov): A collaboration between the Library of Congress and the National Endowment for the Humanities, Chronicling America is a collection of millions of pages of digitized newspapers from across the United States. Articles, headlines, advertisements, comics, and other parts of newspapers can be explored. Search using period-friendly terminology (e.g., automobile instead of car), or explore the Recommended Topics page to see hundreds of different subjects. Be warned that not all recommended topics are appropriate for elementary students.

DOCSTeach (docsteach.org): Sources from the National Archives can be found here and are easily searchable by historical era or format of document. While there are fewer sources here to search, they are more targeted around specific topics and time periods, making it easier to find items if they are digitized. Sources can also be searched by popular topics (docsteach.org/topics), some of which connect to common elementary school topics of study.

Smithsonian Learning Lab (learninglab.si.edu): The Smithsonian Learning Lab brings together digital collections from across the Smithsonian museums. Search results have supporting information about each source. By creating an account and logging in, users are able to save an item to a collection or mark it as a favorite. Users can also access others' collections, making it a very rich and interactive site.

Digital Public Library of America (dp.la): Digital Public Library of America (DPLA) is a portal to search digitized collections from institutions across the country. While they may be found online elsewhere, DPLA allows for a single place to search hundreds of collections of sources. There are several entry points to search and explore, but do not miss the Primary Source Sets listed under Education. There are over a hundred sets organized by topic of study or even literature. Be warned that not every item in a Primary Source Set may actually be a primary source because it was created outside of the time period related to the topic.

TPS Teachers Network (tpsteachersnetwork.org): The TPS Teachers Network is specifically designed for educators who want to explore the use of primary sources in education. Joining the group gives the user access to the TPS Commons, the main group in the network. Teachers can join other groups to target specific interests in using primary sources. Users can post questions, discussions, links, or create albums of primary sources to share with students or colleagues.

Local Institutions: There likely is an institution near your elementary school that holds sources from the past. It may be a museum, public library, or historic organization. It may be within walking distance or a short drive or may be more practical to contact via phone or e-mail.

Students can see the original primary source at local institutions.

Whatever the case, I have always found these institutions invaluable. Not only can they assist in locating primary sources dealing with local history but they can also help take larger themes of history and give them a local significance. Local census records, maps, letters, and photographs can take a historically national event and make it personal because it impacted people who lived long ago in our cities, towns, neighborhoods, or communities.

School Families: Like local institutions, items held as treasures in the homes of school families can give students a personal connection to events that happened years ago. While families may not want treasured keepsakes handled by young children, sharing them digitally with students is a way to provide new value to items that may normally be seen by just a few or hidden in an old shoebox or photo album.

Preparing to Use Primary Sources and This Book

When I prepare to bring primary sources into my library, I think about three things to make the student experience a successful one. One aspect is the analysis strategy that students are going to use. How are they going to interact with the source?

Considerations when preparing to use primary sources in student learning.

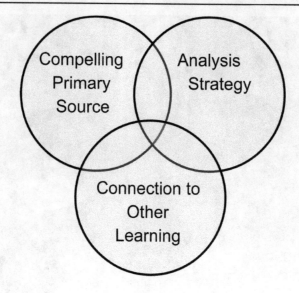

What will they do before, during, and after that interaction? Another consideration is the source itself. What is unique about the primary source that makes it the best item my students can learn from? What is unique about it that I need to consider when thinking about how my students will react and interact with it? A third thought is curricular connections. Why am I bringing primary sources into my students' learning? What other learning does this connect to, and how does that impact how my students learn from the source?

These three considerations do not have to happen in a particular order. I may stumble upon an incredible primary source that begins my thinking about a student learning experience. An analysis strategy may strike me as a great approach for a particular group of students and may begin my thinking about using primary sources with them. I may have a previous lesson that just did not work well and wonder how bringing in a primary source would change the learning. Whatever brings you to consider utilizing primary sources in students' learning, all three of these considerations should be addressed to help the learning be contextual, interactive, and engaging.

This book is arranged to reflect those three entry points. They do not need to be read in order, nor do the sections need to be read from beginning to end. Instead, begin where your current need is. If you lack strategies for your students to analyze a primary source, begin with Chapter 2. If there is a format of primary source that students will be working with or if you struggle to decide what source to choose for students to learn with, look to Chapter 3. If trying to determine how to connect primary source analysis to subject areas, consider Chapter 4. Mastered all of the basics? Chapter 5 goes beyond to assure success for student primary source analysis in the elementary grades. Much like the three considerations for primary source analysis intersect, the three chapters will, when appropriate, reference other chapters of the book.

Chapter 2: "Analyzing Primary Sources in the Elementary Grades" looks at several analysis techniques. It begins with a foundational technique to use with students and building upon that to explore other ways to analyze primary sources. Each will focus on unique aspects of the technique as well as how the technique can be modified for our youngest learners.

Chapter 3: "Selecting Primary Sources" focuses on unique aspects of images, texts, and audiovisual primary sources in analysis. The focus is twofold. First, it considers how educators can introduce and encourage students to explore these unique types of primary sources. Second, the section examines students and their unique interactions with different formats of primary sources.

Chapter 4: Primary source analysis does not exist on its own. "Connecting Primary Sources to Content Curriculum" makes connections between primary source analysis and the four major subject areas of social studies, language arts, science, and math. The chapter explores the purpose behind primary source analysis in the different subject areas and the benefits that can extend to other learning.

Chapter 5: Connecting a curricular need, primary source, and analysis strategy is a strong step to a great experience for students analyzing primary sources. "Assuring Success with Primary Source Analysis: Teacher Tips" takes each of those three considerations steps further by sharing tips that come from years of use as well as distinctive considerations when working with elementary students.

My hope is that as you read this book, you are eager to bring primary sources into your students' learning. Feel free to bring a source, strategy, and connection directly from this book into your classroom, make some element of it your own, or develop a completely new lesson inspired by an aspect of the book. The important thing is that you try something. I can't promise that every attempt will be as successful as you hope. A few of my missteps are in the book, but many more happened. I encourage you to reflect on those missteps and learn from them. Then try again. The power of primary sources will begin to reveal themselves to you and your students!

Chapter 2

Analyzing Primary Sources in the Elementary Grades

I remember the first time I brought primary sources into my elementary class-room. I passed out copies of revolutionary war engravings. I told students what they were, and I waited. I think I expected some magical moment of learning to happen, for students to be amazed by these connections to history. Instead, they didn't know what to do with them. I was losing the moment, but I thought that I could save the lesson. I started telling them why I thought the engravings were important and special. I thought this was a great solution, modeling my thinking for my students so that they could value these pieces of history like I did. I realized later that this wasn't the solution.

Students didn't need to begin by appreciating the primary source. Instead, I needed to give students a framework to look at these primary sources to make sense of them and make meaning from them. They needed to start by analyzing the source. As students analyze a primary source, they find what they value in the source, make connections to other learning, and identify what the source makes them wonder about. I found that I didn't have to model these things; I simply had to give them a structure where they could do it on their own.

I believe the analysis strategy used when working with primary sources is probably the most important of the three considerations when bringing primary sources into an elementary classroom. That may be because of my initial strug-gles, but I think it is also because the analysis is where the magic happens, where students think, learn, wonder, and share in ways that I initially didn't realize they could. This chapter explores several analysis strategies that can be used with elementary students. They come from educators, scholars, and institutions and aren't unique to this book. What is unique are aspects of how they are used with some of our youngest learners.

Considerations when preparing to use primary sources in student learning.

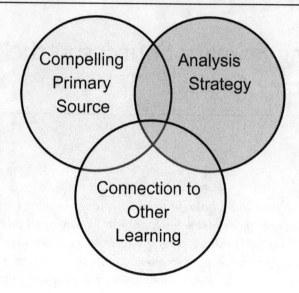

What Happens in Every Primary-Source-Analysis Strategy

There are universal truths that cut across every primary-source-analysis strategy. Knowing them helps teachers and students to understand the common actions that take place in any primary source analysis.

A Teacher Frames the Primary Source Analysis

To a teacher who does more teacher-led instruction, a primary source analysis can feel like students have complete control of their learning and teachers are simply viewing students analyzing primary sources. There can be a feeling of being out of control, and that may not be a good feeling for an educator.

There is some truth to that feeling, but a teacher plays a vital role in primary source analysis in framing the experience and expectations for students. This happens in many ways. Often, the teacher chooses the primary sources that students will interact with. He or she will also provide a statement about the purpose of their learning with the primary source that will focus the attention of students as they begin to look at the source. Along with that focusing statement, the teacher makes choices about what additional information to share about the source. He or she may share when it was created, its title, who its original audience was, or other background information that may give students insight about the source. Whether students will analyze as a whole class, groups, or pairs is determined by the teacher as well. This is how students document and share their analysis with others. How the analysis may be connected with future learning can also be decided by the teacher. For working through an experience that

A teacher frames an analysis to focus students' attention on the primary source.

can feel *out of control*, there are many decisions to be made that impact the experience students will have when analyzing a primary source.

Students Work within the Framework to Analyze the Primary Source

As students analyze a primary source, they are working within the framework that the teacher has provided. Working within that framework gives them opportunities to make their own observations, connections, and questions. As they do this, a teacher may realize that the learning is not going as anticipated. There are things a teacher can do to alter this, but before any changes are made, he or she may want to ask if that is the best course.

Primary source analysis is not a linear path with a clear beginning, middle, and end. Students' work within the framework is not wrong if they are not proceeding along the exact path that the teacher predicted. That framework will focus their attention on parts of the primary source, but it does not predetermine exactly what students will see in the source. Since that student work is not wrong, a teacher may want to reflect on whether it needs to be corrected or if learning is still happening through the analysis, even if it is unanticipated learning.

In fact, many students will go down different paths when analyzing a primary source, developing individual perspectives by focusing on different aspects of a source and making unique personal connections. That does not mean that common learning and understanding do not take place when classes analyze primary sources. In fact, student collaboration during primary source analysis can enrich understanding for everyone.

Students Collaborate through the Analysis

At every grade level, students benefit from interacting with others during primary source analysis. Hearing others' thinking, verbalizing their own thinking, and seeing modeling of the analysis process lead all students toward a richer analysis and deeper connecting, learning, and wondering about the topic under study. Regardless of the grade level, begin with a whole-class collaborative analysis. Some classes may continue analyzing primary sources collaboratively throughout the year. This type of collaborative learning can be the most supportive to students, provide the most opportunities for in-depth thinking, and give teachers the most insight into student thinking.

Collaboration helps give students models for their own thinking.

With whole-class collaboration being a starting point, the following strategies will be described as a whole-class analysis. Alternatives to whole-class collaboration can be implemented as students move toward independent analysis. Keep in mind that independent primary source analysis will likely be a future goal for students as they enter middle or high school. Some form of collaboration during primary source analysis will likely be found in every elementary experience, regardless of how experienced students are with analyzing primary sources. Collaborations during primary source analysis will be explored more in Chapter 5.

Primary Source Analysis Connects to Other Learning

Primary source analysis does not exist in a bubble. Not only does it rely upon students using their prior knowledge to interpret a primary source, it also encourages students to wonder and extend their learning beyond the analysis of the source. In an elementary setting, analyzing a primary source should connect to some aspect of curriculum, preferably both skill and content curriculum.

That connection to curriculum allows students to either come into a primary source analysis with some prior knowledge or later make connections back to their primary source analysis as new learning occurs. These connections come from other resources. Some may be secondary sources, but connecting information from one primary source to another is also beneficial, which will be discussed in Chapter 5.

These common elements of a primary source analysis can allow for rich learning and encourage teachers to consider using an analysis strategy with their students. There are several different approaches to primary source analysis though, each with a slightly different focus. Depending on the learning experience teachers want to create for their students, one may be preferable. There is also something to be said for committing to a primary-source-analysis framework for an extended period of time. It allows the routine of the framework to be understood and internalized by students and may allow them to more easily make connections between one analysis strategy and another as they are introduced to new strategies later.

Strategy 1: See, Think, Wonder Strategy

The See, Think, Wonder strategy was the first primary-source-analysis strategy that I learned, and because of that, I compare all other strategies to this. It originates from Harvard's Project Zero as one of their Visible Thinking strategies and has been paired with the use of primary sources in education by the Library of Congress.

Strategy Overview

See, Think, Wonder asks students to look at a primary source in three ways. They are asked to make observations, naming or identifying things that they see in the primary source. Thinking about the source is reacting to it, making connections, or inferring something from the source. Here, students have an opportunity to bring in their own background knowledge to help them make sense of the primary source. When wondering, students ask questions about the primary source or about the event or person the source is connected to. These questions can help lead them to future learning and other resources.

Framing the See, Think, Wonder Strategy for Students

The teacher will begin framing the analysis by sharing background with students for the analysis. This serves two purposes. First, it connects the learning that will happen through the primary source analysis to other learning that has happened or will happen in the future. Second, it provides a lens students will use to begin the analysis process.

Let's look at an example where second-grade students are studying American symbols. The teacher wants to use a primary source to kick off a lesson on the Statue of Liberty. He or she has found an image of men building the Statue of Liberty (Figure 2.1). It is titled *Workmen constructing the Statue of Liberty in Bartholdi's Parisian warehouse workshop; first model; left hand; and quarter-size head-; Winter 1882?*

Figure 2.1
Workmen Constructing the Statue of Liberty in Bartholdi's Parisian Warehouse Workshop.

There are many ways to frame this analysis. The teacher should consider whether students can likely identify the Statue of Liberty independently, what he or she hopes students discover through the primary source analysis, and how the analysis will connect to other learning. He or she may begin the analysis in any of these ways:

- As we continue to study American symbols, let's analyze this photo of the Statue of Liberty. It's titled *Workmen constructing the Statue of Liberty in Bartholdi's Parisian warehouse workshop; first model; left hand; and quarter-size head-; Winter 1882?* I think it will help us on our journey to uncover why the statue is an American symbol and what it symbolizes.
- Boys and girls, we have been studying American symbols. Today we are going to look at another American symbol, the Statue of Liberty. We are going to analyze a photo of the Statue of Liberty to begin to understand what the statue symbolizes.
- We have been studying American symbols. Today we are going to look at a photo of an American symbol that you may recognize. We will do more than look at the photo though. You are going to analyze it to begin thinking about what elements of America this item symbolizes.
- Boys and girls, I have a photo today connected to our social studies learning. We are going to analyze it to see how it connects to our other learning.

Which of these frameworks best introduces the primary source to students? There is no one right answer. They all frame the primary source analysis differently by giving students different amounts and types of information. That information allows them to make connections to begin their analysis. While there is not a right way to frame the analysis, there are considerations a teacher may make.

Too much information can inhibit students from interacting with a primary source. If students feel like there is no mystery, or nothing to be discovered, they may not fully engage with the source. For example, if students are given the title of the photo, *Workmen constructing the Statue of Liberty in Bartholdi's Parisian warehouse workshop; first model; left hand; and quarter-size head-; Winter 1882?* students have certain information before they look at the photo.

- The American symbol is the Statue of Liberty.
- The photo shows workers building the statue.
- The statue is being built in a warehouse.
- The photo was likely taken in the winter of 1882.

It is unlikely the student will know the name Bartholdi or be familiar with the term "Parisian." They may also not understand the significance of the terms "first model," "left hand," and "quarter-size head." If the teacher is hoping that students will wonder about where the statue is being built, what the men are doing with the statue, or when the Statue of Liberty was built, then giving the title of the photo gives the student too much information.

Of course, giving too little information may also hinder interaction. If a teacher uses the last prompt and simply tells students they will analyze a photo as part of a social studies activity, the students may not have or connect with the background information needed to make meaning from the photo. If the students do not realize that the photo is an American symbol or if they cannot identify the Statue of Liberty, it will be impossible for them to interact with the photo in a meaningful way.

A teacher knowing his or her students' background knowledge on a topic and having an understanding of how he or she wants students to interact with the source can give insight on how to frame the analysis.

Guiding Students through the See, Think, Wonder Strategy

The See, Think, Wonder analysis asks students to do three things: identify observations in the primary source, react to the primary source, and ask questions on the basis of the primary source. These three actions do not happen in isolation. Students will naturally jump from one part of the analysis to another. Assisting and encouraging students to identify what part of the analysis they are working on as they make meaning from the photo is an important part of helping students to learn the strategy.

Guiding Students in Seeing the Primary Source

Beginning with observations allows students to begin their analysis in a very natural way, by looking at the work itself. What may feel new or unnatural at first to students is to do this in a purposeful and collaborative way where what they see is shared with others. Students often keep observations to themselves, sharing their reaction to what they see as opposed to sharing what they are reacting to. A teacher may experience this when students ask a question about classroom learning and the teacher has to stop and ask the students what they are referring to. The students' question can lack the context of the observation that it is based on. The analysis process works to make those individual observations visible to others.

If working with the primary source photo of the building of the Statue of Liberty, after framing the activity, a teacher may prompt students to begin making observations by saying one of the following:

- Look at the photo. Share something that you see.
- What do you see that may be important or interesting?
- What do you see that might help us understand the photo better?

Students will make multiple observations from the photo. As students are becoming more familiar with this strategy, they may begin their response with "I see." To encourage them to do this, the teacher may repeat a student's observation and insert "I see" before it. In addition, the teacher may document the students' observations. This may be done by creating a list on chart paper, documenting what students see on a dry erase or interactive whiteboard, or typing up a list that is projected for students to see. A list created may look something like this:

Tools
Statue
Men with beards
They're all wearing the same thing
Piles of wood
Arm and hand of a statue

Students will likely begin to make inferences on the basis of what they see in the photo. When this happens, document their inference under the *think* category, and push them to make connections with observations or prior knowledge. If a student shares, "I see workers," a teacher may ask, "What do you see that makes you

Students can also write observations on sticky notes.

think they are workers?" This type of question redirects the student back to a supporting observation. If the student points out the men holding hammers, this could be documented under observations.

Students will also make inferences on the basis of personal knowledge. If a student identifies the statue as the Statue of Liberty, a teacher may ask how he or she knows it is the Statue of Liberty. A typical response may be that the student has seen the Statue of Liberty in a book, movie, video, or maybe even in person, and what is seen in the photo looks the same as the Statue of Liberty. When reasonable personal connections are used to inform a student's inference, it should be coupled with an observation. The teacher may ask what the student sees in the photo that makes him or her think this is the Statue of Liberty. Additional observations may include the size of the statue, the draping on the arm, or the tablet being held.

Guiding Students in Thinking about the Primary Source

You may encourage students to think more about the photo by using one of the following prompts:

- You've made a lot of observations. On the basis of those, what do you think is happening in this photo?
- What might the people in the photo have been doing/thinking/saying when this photo was taken?
- Why do you think someone took this photograph?

Like observations, inferences can build on each other as students collaboratively share their thinking. Reactions and inferences to a primary source can vary widely. Some possibilities include the following:

- I think the Statue of Liberty is being built in New York.
- I think the men are building the statue.
- I think the workers are high up building the statue.
- I think the smaller statues were used as models for the real statue.

There are two important things for teachers to keep in mind as students share their thinking about the primary source. First, students will make inferences about the primary source that are incorrect. If it is evident that the inference is based on reasonable evidence and personal knowledge, there is no reason to intervene by correcting or identifying the incorrect thinking. Instead, be sure there are opportunities in student learning to challenge their own thinking by working with other information later as part of another primary source analysis or with secondary sources.

In the photo, the teacher knows that the Statue of Liberty is not being constructed in New York in some elaborate scaffolding, but given what students can see in the photo and what they may know of the statue, these are reasonable inferences about where the photo was taken. Instead of correcting the student, after the primary source analysis, reveal the title of the photo or encourage students to read secondary source text, print or online, about the construction of the statue. Students may return to their primary source analysis and identify those thinking that were confirmed by later learning. This can give the students an opportunity to revisit their thinking and connect them to new learning and can give the teacher an opportunity to check student thinking as students are finding information independently.

When working collaboratively, students will also challenge each other's thinking. When done in an appropriate manner, this can stretch thinking by providing alternative possibilities, show areas where there is no consensus in thinking, and provide opportunities to transform student thinking into student questions.

Guiding Students in Wondering about a Primary Source

Students will begin posing questions as they examine a primary source. In many ways, they are similar to inferences because they are evidence that students are thinking about the source on the basis of the observations and personal connections. Questions that a student pose provide the teacher two major benefits. First, they provide insight into student thinking around areas where there is mystery that piques a student's interest. Second, having insight into student wonderings gives the teacher an opportunity for authentic student learning in the classroom by connecting future learning to student wonderings.

Taken the earlier student thinking, they could easily have been posed as questions.

- I wonder where this photo was taken.
- Are the men building the Statue of Liberty?
- How are the workers using the tools to build the statue?
- Why were the smaller statues built?

Notice that the second and third questions are both related to building the statue. One asks for a simple yes or no, while the other looks for a more complex answer. The teacher may want to work with students to group questions that are alike to encourage deeper thinking about questions without elevating or eliminating student contributions. As students pose questions, other students may attempt to answer them with their own thinking. Both should be documented for future reference, and the teacher may also point out the similarities between these two parts of the analysis process.

Students' questions may lead to later learning.

The teacher may also realize that not all student questions are able to be answered. In the photo example, a student often asks why the two people are standing in the rafters of the building. While reasonable suggestions often follow, as students explore more resources, an answer to this common question is often not found. Be up front about this possibility. A teacher may share the following:

> These are wonderful questions. They're based on what you see in the primary source and show me that you are carefully examining the source. As we look at books, websites, and other sources, hopefully we will find the answer to many questions, but there are some that we might not find answers to. Try not to get stuck looking for one answer to one specific question. You might miss other interesting information about our topic we're studying!

Celebrate with students when they find the answer to a question asked, and encourage students to explore widely within the topic after a primary source analysis. This will help to ensure students feel free to ask a wide variety of questions on the basis of their close observations and their own thinking.

Teacher's Role in the See, Think, Wonder Strategy

The teacher's role in See, Think, Wonder strategy is just as important as the students' roles. The actions a teacher takes support student thinking and guide learning.

Teacher Roles Often Taken On

As students begin the analysis process by making observations, the teacher takes on the role of facilitator. As a facilitator, the teacher may:

- Document student observations
- Inquire or ask for more information about what students see, think, or wonder
- Request observations when students provide reactions or questions
- Make decisions about pacing of analysis
- Encourage transitioning to other parts of the analysis strategy
- Remind students of the framing of the analysis

A teacher can consider himself or herself a guide with students through the analysis process. To guide students, teachers can share the journey ahead by framing the analysis, document the journey through the analysis, and usher students through their analysis. The key thing to keep in mind is that it is the students' analysis and therefore should provide them an opportunity to express their thinking and wondering about the primary source and the topic under study.

One role a teacher often takes on is as a documenter of student thinking. This role works well in a whole-class collaboration. It allows students to focus their attention on the observations, reactions, and questions they are making while also modeling the organization of their thinking. Teacher documentation also helps the pacing of the analysis while maximizing the number of student voices that can be heard.

Another related role is pacing of the primary source analysis. There will likely be a set amount of time allowed for the analysis. Initially, 20 to 25 minutes may be needed. As students become more adept, the analysis will go more quickly. A class with some experience in the See, Think, Wonder strategy may finish a complete analysis as a whole class in 10 minutes. The teacher helps with the pacing and transitioning between focus areas of the analysis.

A teacher also often supports students in clarifying what they are sharing about their thinking. Often a student has thought through observations, reactions, and questions, but he or she struggles to verbalize how they connect. A teacher may ask what observation led to a reaction or question or may ask for more information when students are unclear.

Teacher Roles to Avoid Taking On

Teachers can limit the observations, thinking, and wondering that can happen during a primary source analysis. There are several roles that teachers may typically take on that they should avoid as facilitators. These include the following:

- Confirm student observations as *correct*.
- Explain or teach aspects of the primary source during the analysis.
- Stop students from moving to other parts of the analysis independently.
- Prompt students to guess the teacher's observations, thinking, or questions.
- Ask students to reorganize their own documentation of their analysis.

If a teacher indicates that a student's observation is in some way *right* by agreeing with the student, or even being enthusiastic about the observation, the student may stop his or her own analysis of the primary source and may begin trying to determine what the teacher wants to hear. Also, previous or later sharings by the student may be thought to be in some way wrong because they do not receive the same enthusiasm or approval from the teacher. This isn't to say that the teacher should be robotic but instead can praise the students' efforts as a whole or growth and success in the analysis process. This is challenging to do. Teachers want to connect with students. When a student thinks or acts in a way that a teacher relates to, it is natural to praise or confirm. Keep in mind those students who think differently or who do not connect with the teacher as easily. How does a teacher's actions encourage or discourage them?

Teachers also are used to sharing information, so it is natural for us to want to share knowledge as students begin the process of understanding a primary source or ask a question on the basis of their analysis of the source. The goal here though is for students to uncover understanding and ask questions and then to connect that to other or future learning. Teachers who are going to connect their students to other learning through lecture or historical storytelling should do that after the analysis process, not during it.

Another way a teacher can stifle the thinking and wondering that happen naturally through analysis is to try to compartmentalize it. Students naturally analyze. They make observations, react and interpret, and ask questions. Put something new in front of a group of kindergarten students, and you will hear all three of those within seconds, and the observations, reactions, interpretations, and questions will all be intertwined. The purpose of formalizing the analysis in the See, Think, Wonder strategy is to have deeper and more meaningful observations, thinking, and wonderings. We do this by identifying and organizing our analysis, but to only allow one part of the analysis to happen at a time goes against the instinctive nature students have.

As students begin to work in smaller collaborative groups, they will also document their own analysis. It is inevitable that most students will mix up observations,

Do not worry about placement of thinking from analysis. What is important is deep thinking.

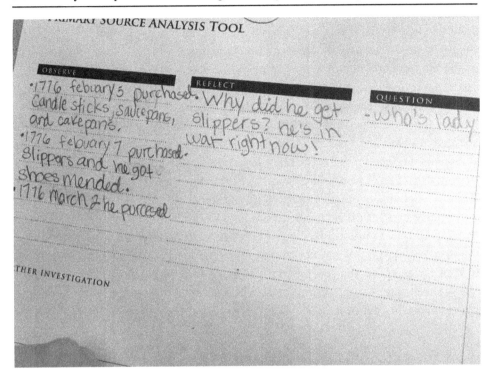

reactions, and questions as they document their own thinking. Typically, this is because they are trying to write down thoughts that are coming quickly. Also, we rarely organize our thinking this way, so it is a new skill they are practicing. Ultimately, what is important is that they are making meaningful observations, reactions, and questions. If the teacher would stop the students and ask them to erase or reorganize their thinking, it slows down the analysis. Instead, rely on modeling, and if a student is chronically having issues with organizing his or her thinking, the teacher may want to provide a different organizational tool or bring it to the student's attention as something that can be worked on in future analysis.

Teacher Roles Sometimes Taken On

There are other roles that teachers should do sparingly. They can assist students as they learn the See, Think, Wonder strategy, but if they are done too often, it can inhibit students from taking ownership of their own analysis. These roles are the following:

- Model the analysis process by sharing their own observations, thoughts, and questions.
- Redirect students when their focus on the primary source moves away from the topic under study.

Modeling can be an important step the first or even second time for students using any primary-source-analysis strategy, including See, Think, Wonder. Students can benefit from the language and methods shown by the teacher. Modeling should be used sparingly though because it can quickly turn students into trying to match the teacher's thinking in addition to the process he or she is trying to demonstrate. To assist those students who may learn the strategy more slowly, the teacher can consider performing the analysis as a whole class. This allows opportunities for the teacher to model an aspect of the strategy, and then students who are ready to embrace a part of the strategy become models for other students. This also gives the teacher an opportunity to acknowledge language or process that a student uses. For example, saying, "I like how you started your observation with 'I see,'" encourages other students to do the same.

Students can get offtrack during the See, Think, Wonder strategy. This often happens in one of two ways. One possibility is students focusing on aspects of the primary source that are not important to the learning that the teacher hopes will take place from the analysis. In the image of the Statue of Liberty, students may concentrate their attention on the silhouettes in the rafters in the top of the photo. There is a lot of mystery in that aspect of the photo. Who are they? What

Modeling language can encourage students to use it in their own analysis.

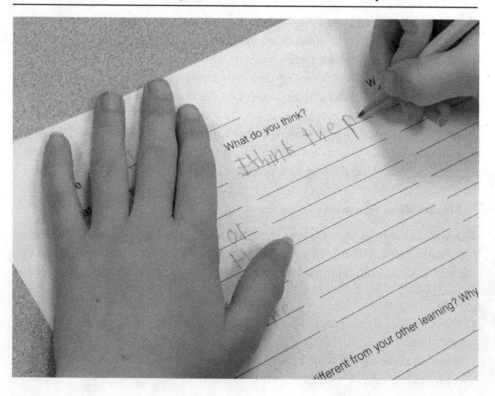

are they doing there? How did they get up there? The second way that students can become lost during the analysis process is by misidentifying parts of an image while making observations. In our example photo, there is a latticed framework that was used in the building of the statue. Students often misidentify these pieces as ladders. That can lead to them wondering or speculating what the ladders were used for. It is unlikely that any of these speculations, questions, or the answers to them lead to the learning about the statue.

If a teacher anticipates an analysis going astray, he or she may try to address this in the framing of the analysis. If all else fails, reframing the analysis and reminding students what the purpose of the analysis is can help refocus the analysis. That being said, there is not one correct road to get to learning through primary source analysis. Teachers can consider paying close attention to students' observations, reactions, and questions while also giving them some leeway to see if they self-correct if taken off course.

Differentiating the See, Think, Wonder Strategy for Youngest Learners

The See, Think, Wonder strategy can be used with very young learners. Teachers may want to think about three elements in planning their analysis with these students: the source, working collaboratively, and students documenting their thinking. All of these considerations revolve around reading and writing since our youngest learners are often emerging readers and writers.

Consider using image- or video-based primary sources where students will not have to interact with text or will have to interact with very little text. This may include formats such as photos, drawings, paintings, maps, newspaper images or image-based advertisements, audios such as short interviews, and videos or films such as commercials or actuality films. In Chapter 3, we will explore special considerations for using some of these different formats. Think about seeking them out for younger learners.

As our youngest learners analyze primary sources as part of their learning, a teacher may also consider the type of collaboration used. As stated earlier, collaborative analysis can lead to expanded thinking as a student hears another student's thinking. Just as important for younger learners, collaborative analysis allows for constant modeling by other students and monitoring by the teacher facilitating the analysis. As these students become more familiar with the See, Think, Wonder strategy, a teacher may want to encourage smaller collaborative opportunities, such as a Turn and Talk with a fellow student, ultimately bringing the sharing back to a whole-class setting.

While many younger students will verbally share their seeing, thinking, and wondering with a whole group, there can be benefits to personally documenting

Collaborative analysis may happen in small groups before students check in as a whole class.

prior to sharing or during sharing. With emerging writers, using the Primary Source Analysis Tool from the Library of Congress would be frustrating. Instead, with primary source images, consider giving students copies of the primary source to write on. Students can circle, underline, or otherwise annotate things they see in the primary source. This will give the teacher an understanding of where students are focusing their attention prior to sharing and will give students the autonomy to document other students' findings as they are shared with the class. Other icons such as arrows, question marks, or sight words can be used to show connections, questions, or observations by emerging writers.

Strategy 2: Close Reading Strategy

Many districts or schools use a close reading strategy to use with fiction or informational nonfiction text. Close reading can also be used as an effective primary-source-analysis strategy when working with text-based primary sources. The use of the Close Reading strategy with primary sources was inspired by my reading of Christopher Lehman and Kate Roberts's book *Falling in Love with Close Reading*. While that book does not specifically mention the use of primary source text, the pairing of historical text with the strategy seemed to open possibilities to student understanding.

Its simple and straightforward approach makes it a good choice when pairing with primary sources. If a student is already familiar with another close reading strategy though, adapting that to analyze primary sources may be a better approach for him or her.

Strategy Overview

Close Reading with primary sources is limited to text-based formats, such as letters, newspapers, or diaries, but can also be used with transcribed audio formats, such as recorded interviews or speeches. The three-step process asks students to read a primary source through a particular lens, to use that lens to uncover patterns in the primary source, and finally to work with the patterns to uncover new understanding.

Framing the Close Reading Strategy for Students

Teachers play a critical role in framing the analysis by giving students a lens in which to view the primary source. Like other primary-source-analysis strategies, the Close Reading strategy empowers students to make decisions about where they focus their attention within the primary source and synthesize the patterns they find to draw meaning from the source. The lens the teacher provides the class guides students through the primary source analysis. This does not mean all students will see the primary source in the same way. Instead, it allows a teacher to predict how a student's analysis will connect with other classroom learning. Also, a shared lens makes collaborative work between students more meaningful because it is more likely a student will make connections to another classmate's thinking.

As an example, let's look at a series of advertisements for chocolate and other sweets in newspapers from the 1910s and 1920s (Figures 2.2 and 2.3). This may be used as part of a larger learning unit on nutrition or as an authentic learning experience on perspective and message in advertising.

For our example, the lesson topic will be perspective and message in advertising. To provide a lens and begin the analysis process, a teacher may share with the class the following (see Figures 2.2 and 2.3):

> When a company wants to sell you something, they do more than just show you the item they want you to buy. They often try to make you feel or think something about it, and to do that, people who create advertisements choose their words carefully. This has been happening for a long time. Today, we're going to look at advertisements that were in newspapers over one-hundred years ago. We are going to use a Close Reading strategy to analyze the ads.

Figure 2.2
November 7, 1922, *Public Ledger.*

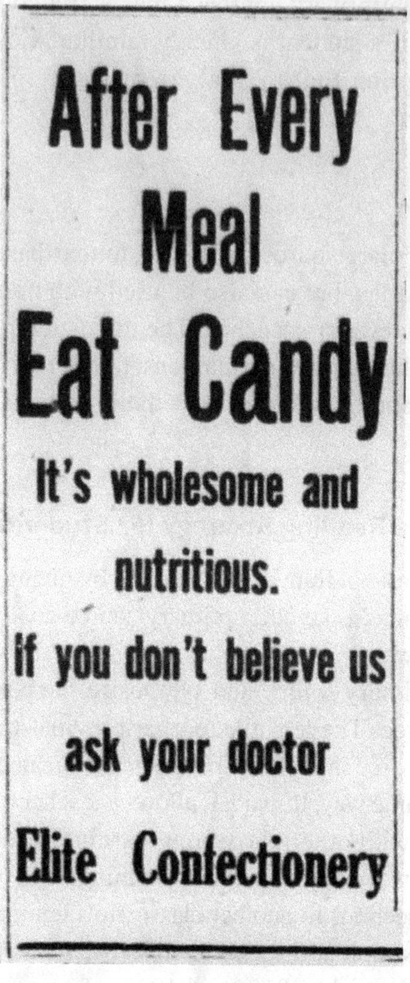

After Every
Meal
Eat Candy
It's wholesome and
nutritious.
If you don't believe us
ask your doctor
Elite Confectionery

The first step in our strategy is to view the text through a special lens. Using a lens will help you focus in on certain parts of the text. For our advertisements, let's use the lens of word choice. What words in the advertisement jump out to you? What words or short phrases get your attention?

Notice that, in this example, the teacher gives very little information about the sources. The only additional information is that the texts are newspaper advertisements and when they were created. Identifying them as advertisements helps to establish the purpose, connecting this work to prior knowledge of advertisements in a variety of formats. Identifying when they were created, since that information is not necessarily important to the learning, takes away any wondering that students may have about when these items were created that may distract from the analysis.

Figure 2.3
September 25, 1919, *Evening Public Ledger.*

This allows the student to have an initial interaction with the text that is shaped primarily by the lens that the teacher sets and by the student's prior knowledge.

Guiding Students through the Close Reading Strategy

Students navigate through a three-step process when analyzing a primary source with the Close Reading strategy (Figure 2.4). While there can be opportunity to jump between these steps, it is more likely they will follow a linear path through the analysis process. In the first step, they use the lens set by the teacher to interact with the text, identifying parts of the text according to that lens. In the second step, students organize the identified text, looking for patterns and labeling those patterns. Finally, students construct new knowledge on the basis of the patterns they have found. This can be used with a variety of text-based primary sources and a number of lenses.

Guiding Students to Read through a Lens

The three-step process begins with students reading the primary source text through a lens. In our example from the earlier section, advertisements will be

Figure 2.4
Close Reading Steps.

| Read Through a Lens | ▶ | Find Patterns In the Text | ▶ | Create New Understanding |

---

read through the lens of word choice. The number of lenses are endless and should be tailored to what the teacher wants students to focus on in the text. Other lens choices that may be used with this particular grouping of primary sources are a lens looking for a point of view or a lens that looks for text evidence to support a specific claim.

As students read the text of the advertisement, one way to keep them fully engaged with the text is to write directly on the source, underlining, circling, or otherwise marking words and phrases that they are choosing as strong word

---

Students may be more engaged in analysis when writing directly on a source.

choices. In this case, there are several advertisements that students are working with, so two students may have different primary sources they are working with. Pairing students together may also be a choice, especially as students are new to this analysis strategy.

After students have had sufficient time to read and annotate the source, ask students what words or phrases they identified while they were looking through the lens of word choice. In this group, students may have identified words and phrases like these:

Wholesome
Nutritious
Twenty-four hours fresh
Desire
Do you realize
Chocolate

In this example, there are multiple related primary sources used, and each student or pair of students may look at a couple of them. In other cases, all students may be reading the same primary source. It is important for students to know that they do not all have to agree on what words or phrases were selected when viewing the primary source text through the lens. Instead, they should be able to give some explanation about why they chose the word or phrase if asked. Students here may have shared that they selected words that jumped out at them; that were unexpected, new, or unfamiliar to them; or that seemed to get the person reading the advertisement to think.

The first concern of some teachers is that their students chose words when viewing the primary source through the lens that the teacher didn't select. Do not worry. Those rogue words and phrases will typically be dealt with in the next step. The other possibility is that there may be more to the sources than anticipated by the teacher. This can lead to a more interesting discussion as students reveal their thinking.

In the example, students are wrestling with issues of point of view or bias within text, but they could be searching for a central idea or defining words on the basis of surrounding context. It is all dependent on what the teacher wants the students' focus to be and therefore what lens he or she asks them to look through when reading the text.

Guiding Students through Finding Patterns

After identifying and sharing words or phrases from the text while viewing through a lens, students move on to the second step of the Close Reading strategy, finding a pattern or patterns among the group of words and phrases and describing that pattern.

We began by focusing on word choice in these advertisements. Now, I'd like you to take the collection of words and find a pattern or patterns. How can we group some of these words together? And how would we describe the group?

There are some important things to know about finding patterns using this strategy. You do not have to use every word and if you are making multiple groups, a word can appear in different groups.

Take a few minutes to work with a partner on this. Discuss what words should be placed together and why they should be together. Then we'll share with the whole class.

Having students work in pairs or small groups helps in a couple ways. First, it encourages students to start vocalizing their thinking as they find a pattern, a useful experience when they have to name the pattern soon after. Second, it supports students who may be more hesitant to move from identification to pattern recognition. There will be students who will readily point out words that, in this case, jump out at them but stop short at trying to explain why to the teacher. Hearing modeling from another student and having a chance to practice that explanation with a student can ease the reluctant student into the second step of the primary source analysis.

As students begin their groupings of words, some may want to go back to the original text and look for additional words and phrases that support the pattern of words they are identifying. Certainly, after students can describe the pattern of words, finding other supporting text within the primary source not only helps students strengthen their argument for the pattern they are illustrating but also helps them to further define their ideas around this text. If time permits, encourage students to revisit the primary source text, circling back to step one with a more targeted reading through a lens that they have created.

In our example, students I have worked with identify one or two groups. The most typical group has to do with chocolate being described as *healthy*. In that group, students may place the following words and phrases:

- Wholesome
- Nutritious
- Ask your doctor
- Pure
- Natural and healthy

Another pattern is sometimes found that students label as *words and phrases that try to persuade or sell*. This list of words may include the following:

- Ask your doctor
- The standard
- The gift the whole world loves

- Wife or mother would rather have
- Teach them to enjoy it

A teacher may initially be concerned about two things during this part of the analysis. First, students may not use all of the identified words from the first stage of analysis as they are identifying patterns. Just as the teacher may encourage students to return to the original primary source text to find additional support for their patterns, a teacher should also know that not everything students initially identify is helpful to them in making meaning from the text. Second, students may not identify the patterns that the teacher hopes or describe the pattern in the way the teacher expects. It may be helpful to remember that primary source analysis gives students an opportunity to have ownership of their learning and to celebrate the ownership they are taking of it.

If students are struggling with identifying patterns after reading the text through a lens, a teacher may want to revisit the original lens students viewed the text through, the selection of the primary source text itself, or how vocabulary and readability of the text could be supported. Students may be grouping text in ways that make sense but can struggle with naming the pattern that they find. Having discussions with pairs, small groups, or the entire class about why a group of words and phrases were placed together may help some students in verbalizing their thinking.

Guiding Students through Developing Understanding

The final stage of the Close Reading strategy is for students to develop understanding. After reading the primary source text through a lens to identify important parts of the text and looking for patterns in the text they identify, what meaning can they make from that level of analysis? For students in middle or high school, the sophisticated task of being able to verbalize the learning may come more easily. For elementary students, it can be done, but much like the teacher framed the initial analysis task by defining the lens, question prompts may help students transition into thinking about the learning that has taken place.

A teacher likely begins this primary-source-analysis strategy knowing where he or she would like the students to end up, but what he or she initially will not know is where the students will be at this point in the analysis. Did students identify the text that the teacher expected? If not, then the teacher needs to be flexible, not in altering the thinking and learning the students have already done but in how he or she helps students transition to the final stage of analysis. To determine this, a teacher may ask himself or herself: "What open-ended questions can I pose to help students describe their findings from the primary source analysis and connect it to the context that I introduced at the beginning of the lesson?"

Student shows her deep understanding of the text through her close reading analysis.

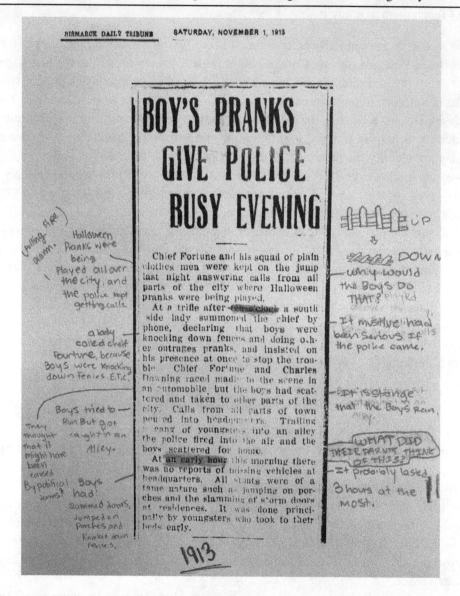

Let's return to part of the introduction to this analysis:

When a company wants to sell you something, they do more than just show you the item they want you to buy. They often try to make you feel or think something about it, and to do that, people who create advertisements choose their words carefully.

If students' analysis went as the teacher expected, he or she may simply be able to repeat or return to this part of the introduction. The teacher may follow this with:

Does this appear to be true or false based on the group of advertisements that you analyzed? Tell me more about that. How do you know?

Students more experienced in this analysis strategy may need even less prompting. They may be transitioned into the final stage of analysis by asking:

As we have looked through the lens of *word choice* and found patterns in the words we identified, what did we discover about this grouping of advertisements? And what could that tell us about advertisements in general?

Other students who are striving to make those connections between analysis and learning may benefit from talking through the analysis stages to transition into describing new understandings.

However students are led to verbalize that new understanding, they should be expressing new ideas about the text that they have read as well as the topic under study. Those new ideas will be rooted in the observations made in the text and the patterns discovered. Prompts can further assist students in sharing their new understanding. Examples of these will be explored later in this chapter when looking at using Visible Thinking strategies in exit slips.

The three-step Close Reading strategy gives students an opportunity to interact with text and to share their unique interactions and understandings with the teacher and the class. It is so much more than simply reading a primary source letter, newspaper article, or diary entry. This strategy encourages careful observation of words and phrases in a way that is supported by the teacher and peers throughout to assure success and new understanding by the students.

Teacher's Role in the Close Reading Strategy

At the beginning of the Close Reading strategy, a teacher has the opportunity to frame the strategy through the lens. During that stage, he or she takes a supportive role to assure that students are successfully interacting with the primary source text.

Teacher Roles Often Taken On

Leading up to and during the Close Reading strategy, a teacher may be found:

- Selecting the primary source text or texts that students will interact with
- Setting the direction of the analysis by providing the students a lens to view the primary source
- Defining words or phrases to help students make sense of historical text
- Collecting student findings to help facilitate analysis across the class

The initial selection of the primary source text as well as the lens that students will view that text through is critical for elementary students' success using the Close Reading strategy as a primary source analysis. The teacher will want to preview the source text looking at issues such as message, vocabulary, readability, and length to determine how successful his or her students will be in understanding the text. Then, he or she will choose a lens in which to read the text, encouraging students to focus on a specific aspect of the primary source to lead to new student knowledge and ultimately to connect to other learning. These choices, which take place prior to the students analyzing the text, are critical to the success of the strategy.

Some primary source text may have vocabulary that is unfamiliar to students. Not only may language be new to developing readers but other words may also be dated or unique to a specific event or time period. Challenging vocabulary should not stop an engaging piece of primary source text from being used. Instead, the teacher can provide a glossary for the document, connect new vocabulary to related images, or introduce the new words in another way to assure that students will be able to successfully read the text.

As a class works collaboratively through the Close Reading strategy, a teacher often will document student findings, display student-created groupings, and visibly show connections students are making verbally. As a teacher documents students' thinking and learning, he or she may also point out the steps in the process to help students transition their thinking from one stage of analysis to another. As students become more familiar with the strategy, students may begin transitioning independently through the analysis process.

Teacher Roles to Avoid Taking On

To continue to support a student's independent thinking, a teacher facilitating the Close Reading strategy will want to avoid actions that limit a student's ability to interact with the text and develop his or her own knowledge on the basis of those interactions.

While well intentioned, a teacher may want to avoid:

- Identifying words or phrases that the teacher finds important to understanding the text
- Arranging findings to reveal a pattern of information in the text
- Telling students what their new understanding should be on the basis of their analysis

The key to the Close Reading strategy is for students to engage in the text. While a modeling of a single interaction may assist students in beginning their own analysis, a teacher should not *fill in the gaps* by pointing out text or phrases that, according to the teacher, the students missed. In a related fashion, the teacher should allow students to find patterns from the text as well as new understandings on the basis of those patterns. This isn't to say that a teacher does not come in with a well-timed question to assist a student in verbalizing his or her thinking or to model, but as a colleague of mine often says, "Don't steal their struggle."

A teacher may feel the urge to step in because students are not finding the text or patterns that he or she expected them to. Instead of taking on the student role, revisit the teacher's role. Examine the lens that students were tasked with. Does it encourage students to find the text you want them to focus on, or is there a related lens that should be used? Are there questions or other prompts that you could have provided that might have guided students' attention when analyzing the primary source? Are there pockets of students who did not target the expected text where collaboration or vocabulary support could have played a role?

The teacher should be open to the happy miscalculation that students are engaging with the text in different ways than expected. What new learning does that lead to, and how does that learning connect to the students' learning objectives and other learning related to the primary source analysis? These connections, because they are led by students, can sometimes be more meaningful than what the teacher had anticipated.

Teacher Roles Sometimes Taken On

A teacher may perform other actions sparingly, especially as students are becoming familiar with the Close Reading strategy when used as a primary-source-analysis tool. These interactions between teachers and students should not only assist in the immediate primary source analysis but also be used as a model as students move toward more independent analysis.

To help students verbalize their thinking, a teacher will sometimes:

• Label patterns of text when students are unable to do so
• Question students' findings to help them make their thinking visible
• Assist students in transitioning their thinking as they progress through the analysis strategy

A teacher will unsurprisingly find that he or she needs to provide more support as students first encounter the Close Reading strategy as a form of primary source analysis. While an engaging primary source and prompt will help students engage with the text, they may initially struggle to verbalize or label that thinking. Because they will be connecting that thinking to past or future learning, verbalization is an important part to primary source analysis and should be practiced and modeled when necessary.

As students begin to organize words or phrases identified during the analysis, some may find it difficult to label groupings or explain why they are grouped the way they are. Their teacher may assist with that labeling, being sure to confirm with students that the title or reasoning given to a group of text represents what students are thinking. Another way to lead students to an understanding of how to arrange text is to question why they initially selected the text. Asking a student how the text he or she selected relates to the lens that was introduced can give both the teacher and the student insight into the student's thinking. Finally, because each step of this analysis strategy is more distinct than some other strategies, the thinking that takes place is also distinct. Providing students with a transitional think aloud to target their thinking during the transition can help some students move from one type of thinking to the next.

Differentiating the Close Reading Strategy for Youngest Learners

A teacher will likely not use the Close Reading strategy with his or her youngest students who are early emergent readers because of the need to be able to interact with text. This should not dissuade a teacher from using the strategy with students who are reading independently or are striving readers. If students can read text, they can interact with it, and modifications to this strategy can ensure that a young reader can come to a deeper understanding of the text than he or she would be able to by simply reading it.

Think about the type, length, and vocabulary in a primary source text. Just like other text young learners will interact with, choosing shorter primary source text with accessible vocabulary may allow students to make meaning from it. These shorter texts may be found in newspaper headlines, or consider choosing a small portion of a full primary source text. Instead of a letter, consider whether one short paragraph shows students the intentions of the writer or some other aspect worth investigating.

Consider text that is accompanied by imagery as a way to support success in reading comprehension. Pictures can support students in understanding primary source text and are a way to allow younger readers to interact with the text successfully. Captions or advertisements in newspapers are one way to bring in short pieces of primary source text with visual support. The text can also be paired with primary source images to help students visualize as they are using the Close Reading strategy.

Predict students' work through the first two stages of the strategy to determine whether a specific group's interaction with a specific text is developmentally appropriate. Predicting student responses is always helpful in planning the support that can be provided, but it is even more so when thinking about the youngest learners. Those predictions can help a teacher plan how to alter prompts or model support to help his or her students reveal their own thinking. Be sure that the new learning you are hoping students obtain at the end of the strategy is achievable with some level of independence. If not, using different primary sources or even a different primary-source-analysis strategy may be in order. Remember that one of the goals in primary source analysis is for students to be able to express their own thinking. Too much support can lead to students simply answering predetermined prompts that lead them down a narrow path of answers instead of a wider road of possible outcomes as students show some independence in their thinking.

Strategy 3: See, Wonder, Think Strategy

One of the powers of a well-selected primary source is that it makes students wonder. There are times, through analysis, that a teacher may want students to focus on analyzing a primary source as a way for them to develop their own questions. This may be done as an introduction to a unit of study or a particular lesson that will connect with other resources. Students generating their own research questions may be another reason primary sources are used in this way.

While the See, Think, Wonder strategy can help students generate questions, using a similar See, Wonder, Think strategy can shift the analysis to focus on the questions that students think of related to the primary source.

Strategy Overview

The See, Wonder, Think strategy makes one change to See, Think, Wonder. This change alters the focus of students, guiding them to generate questions on the basis of their observations and then begin to think of possible responses to the questions. The strategy feels familiar to students who have used See, Think, Wonder. That familiarity may make it an appealing choice. It also may make it a strategy that requires less modeling from a teacher.

Framing the See, Wonder, Think Strategy for Students

One difference between the See, Think, Wonder strategy and the shift to focus on students thinking of their own questions in the See, Wonder, Think strategy is that students know that the purpose for examining the primary source is to ask questions on the basis of the source. One similarity between the two is the selection of a primary source as a focus. This teacher's role of selecting the primary source becomes even more important when its purpose is to ask questions as the focus of the analysis. For our illustrative example, we will use a photo taken by Lewis Hine (Figure 2.5) that is part of the National Child Labor Committee Collection held at the Library of Congress. There may be several places in an elementary curriculum that a teacher may want to choose this photo to ask students to generate questions. Maybe there is a unit on people's rights or, more specifically, children's rights. There may be a study on current stories around child labor. In either case, these

Figure 2.5
Seven-year-old Alex Reiber Topping.

could be used for a historical perspective. For our example, students will be in a unit in an early grade comparing life today to life long ago, looking back at moments in history. When selecting a photo or other primary source that will focus on questions, it is helpful for a teacher to put himself or herself in the role of the student. Looking at the primary source, the following questions may be considered:

- What parts of the image or text stand out?
- What elements of the image or text will be recognizable to students? What will not?
- What basic questions might students initially ask about this primary source?
- What more complex questions might a student ask?
- What resources do I have to help answer those possible questions?

Noticing what stands out will give the teacher an idea of where the students will place their attention. Those places in the photo, in this example, may also be the basis on which questions are formed. In this photo, a student might first be drawn to the items in the child's hands. Other elements like the setting or the clothing or even the person may be things that are noticed second. The teacher may anticipate that an initial question could include, "What is in the boy's hands?"

Identifying what students will see as recognizable and unrecognizable will also help when selecting a primary source. With a text-based source, look for words, phrases, and descriptions that students will connect or struggle with. In an image, look for individuals, backgrounds, and items. If there is too much that is unfamiliar, students may be unable to go beyond the basic questions of "Who/what/where is this?" If everything is familiar, students may struggle to wonder about the primary source.

One element of classroom instruction that comes into play is what background the students have for the topic under study. Sometimes, providing some background before the See, Wonder, Think strategy or waiting to teach about some aspects of an event until after the primary source analysis may help students connect to a primary source while still finding elements that are unfamiliar. In the example, a younger student may identify the item in the boy's left hand as a vegetable, although he or she likely will not know that it is a sugar beet. The student may not even know what a beet or sugar beet is. Because of the position of the hand holding the knife, the teacher may anticipate that the student will make an educated guess that the child in the photo is holding a knife.

With an idea of what students will identify and struggle to identify, a teacher may then look at the type of questions that a student may ask. Consider both basic and complex questions that may be asked. These will vary by the age of student and familiarity with elements of the primary source. For this source, students may ask:

Is this a boy or a girl?
Who is the boy?
Where are his parents?
What is he holding? Is it a knife?
Is that a bunch of carrots?
Why is he cutting the plant out in the field?
Is that knife sharp?
When was this picture taken?
Where was this picture taken?
Who took this picture?
Why did someone take this picture?

On the basis of these possible questions, the teacher wants to ask himself or herself whether these can lead to learning that would meet the objectives of the lesson or unit. Part of that consideration are the available resources to answer these questions. Consider both other primary sources and secondary source text.

In the See, Wonder, Think strategy, there is a structure that can be shared as part of the framing of the activity. The teacher may even draw upon students' experiences with the related See, Think, Wonder strategy.

Today, as we continue to explore the past, let's look at what life was like for one boy about your age. This photo that we will look at was taken about one hundred years ago. We are going to use it to begin wondering about what life was like for children back then. To do that, you are going to ask your own questions that we can explore after looking at this photo.

We are going to use a new strategy called See, Wonder, Think. It sounds similar to the See, Think, Wonder strategy you already know and there are some similarities. Like See, Think, Wonder, you will start by pointing out things in the photo that you see. Focus some of your time on pointing out things that are unusual or unknown. As you notice things about the primary source, begin to ask questions about them. What do you wonder about? What would you ask the person in the photo or the person who took the photo? What seems different from a child's life today that you may want to know more about? As you ask questions or after you ask questions, begin to think about possible answers to those questions or what you know that is related to the question.

Take a look at our photo. When you are ready to share something that you see, raise your hand and start sharing. I'll be in charge of writing questions down.

The teacher has done two things here that are worth noting. The first is that he or she has shared some information about the photo with the students to set the purpose of the analysis and of choosing the photo. The teacher shares that the child in the photo is around the same age as the students and that the photo was taken about 100 years ago. While he or she eliminates a couple of questions that students may have asked on their own, the questions are basic, and it may make sense to share the information to give the activity context and help students connect with the primary source. The second thing the teacher has done is to take on the role of recorder. With this young group, it makes sense to record information so that the time writing can pace the time thinking and sharing. This may not make sense in older elementary grades, especially if students are working in small groups and not as a whole class.

The See, Wonder, Think strategy asks students to begin by making observations and naming them. Because it is related to a familiar strategy, framing See, Wonder, Think can reference the See, Think, Wonder not only to draw upon connections to that analysis strategy but also to point out differences from it.

Guiding Students through the See, Wonder, Think Strategy

The See, Wonder, Think strategy asks students to make observations, create questions on the basis of those observations and their own knowledge, and give a reasonable answer to that question or identify what they would need to find the answer to that question. The process is more linear than the See, Think, Wonder strategy although students may find themselves not working in a linear path as they document their thinking.

Guiding Students in Seeing the Primary Source

Students begin the See, Wonder, Think strategy much like they do See, Think, Wonder, by observing the primary source. In the case of a visual primary source, the teacher may begin by prompting students to make observations. He or she may tell students the following:

Take a close look at this photo. What do you recognize? What is new to you? Is there anything that you cannot identify or that seems out of place? What here makes you wonder?

The prompt, along with the framing of the analysis, initially encourages students to think about asking questions. Working off a three-column organizer, students can document their observations. Whole-class observations may be captured on an interactive whiteboard or poster-size reproduction of the primary source.

In our example, students will likely make several initial observations. Working collaboratively, a student may make a new observation on the basis of another student's earlier observation. These could include:

Boy
Tool
Knife
Plant
Carrot
Hat
Field
House
Glove
Pants
Shirts
Black-and-white photo
Torn edges

As students continue to make observations, some students may begin asking questions before being prompted. This may be because of the teacher's framing of the strategy or because an observation he or she made or heard from another student prompted a question. Do not dismiss those questions by telling students that it is not time to ask questions yet. There is never a time not to share a question during this strategy! Thank the student, write down the question, and continue taking observations from the students.

The only time a teacher may stop to follow up with a student is if it is not obvious to the teacher what the student is basing the question on. For example, if a student asks, "Where are the boy's parents?" and no one had voiced an observation about the boy being in the field alone, a teacher may want to inquire.

"That's an interesting question. As I look over at our observations, I'm not sure we have written down what you are seeing that makes you wonder that." If the student struggles to verbalize the observation, the teacher may ask other students for help or may model voicing the observation, confirming with the original student that a particular part of the primary source being observed was a basis for his or her question.

There may be disagreements as students make observations. For example, one student may think that what they see in the photo are carrots, another student may think it is a beet, and another may not know what it is but disagree with the first two students. If this happens, encourage the students to turn their disagreement into a question. To question the primary source is one important point of this primary source analysis!

I'm hearing that there is some disagreement about what we see in this photo. That can happen, especially when we look at a primary source where there is something that we are unfamiliar with. Instead of writing down all three, let's label this part of the photo with a question mark. That will tell us that we need to come back and ask a question about this part of the photo.

The question can be written in a variety of ways:

- Are these carrots?
- Is this a potato?
- What kind of vegetable is this?
- What is this?

There is not one correct question here. What is important is that the students are curious and becoming invested in an aspect of the photo. Regardless of the question, when they find the answer to be a beet, a likely next question could be, "Why is the boy cutting a beet in the middle of a field?" Give all involved in the original disagreement a chance to voice their question or take ownership of a question someone else already asked.

Do not be concerned if there are misconceptions at this point. These observations, such as a student thinking that they are seeing carrots, may become a question, especially if challenged by another student. If it is not challenged, there will be another opportunity for the student to clarify his or her thinking.

Guiding Students in Wondering about the Primary Source

To transition from observations to questions, the teacher wants to tap into his or her students' sense of wonder. This can be challenging. Students typically only raise their hand when they have an answer, not necessarily to show what they do not know. There may be several ways to encourage students to voice their own wonder related to a primary source.

- There are many observations here. Some of them look like things you may see every day. Others are things that maybe you only see once in a while. Think about those things that you do not see, read about, or talk about every day. It is difficult to be experts on those things. Can anyone see something here that they do not see every day?
- I see this photo and there are things I understand about it, but there are other things that I'm not quite sure about. Those things make me wonder, make me ask questions. I'm wondering if you have some questions about this photo too.
- You have pointed out so many things you see in this photo. All of those observations make me wonder about the person in the photo, the person who took the photo, and about how this boy's life is the same or different from yours today. We even have a few questions, telling me there are already people wondering about those things. Who else is wondering about some part of this person's story? What would you want to ask?
- There are so many things to see in this photo, but that does not tell us everything. I'm wondering about what I might ask the boy in the photo if I could speak to him. What if I could speak to people he knew? What would I ask? I'm thinking about what questions I would have for the person who took the photo. What I'm really wondering is what you would ask any of these people if you could.

It is difficult to choose just one way to encourage students to push them toward thinking about questions. These are just a few, but any teacher may already have a

A teacher may have students write observations and questions in different colored sticky notes on a projected image.

way that he or she encourages students to question that would work just as well in this transition.

Depending on the groups students are working in, the teacher or students may be documenting their own questions. Whatever the situation, encourage students to write down or share as many questions as possible. They should not be self-editing their questions at this point. Think of it more as a brainstorming session. To that end, be prepared. Do not let the end of a list or not enough space on a board give students a visual cue that they should wrap up their wondering. Make spaces larger than you think they could ever need. They may surprise you when given the task.

While sharing questions, it is inevitable that a student will try to answer someone else's question. That student may have some background knowledge that others do not. Possibly, they simply see the primary source in a different way. Just as when students ask questions while others are observing, document these thoughts. A teacher may tell a student: "That is a possible answer to the question. Let's write that down here so that we can return to it later."

While the teacher is working to organize the thoughts students share, he or she also does not want to stifle them. This is a difficult road to walk. Ultimately, the teacher should look to the students and make a judgment about whether all students are not only having the opportunity to share but also encouraged to do so.

One may hope that the questions span a vast range. The teacher may model a type of question if he or she feels students are missing an element of analyzing the photo. For example, if students are only focused on the boy in the photo, the teacher may model the thinking that leads to asking a question about the person who took the photo by asking, "I hear a lot of great questions about the boy in the photo. I'm also wondering about the person who took the photo and thinking about a question I may ask him."

Guiding Students in Thinking about the Primary Source

As questions become exhausted, students will move to the *Think* portion of the strategy. Here, teachers have a decision to make and may choose to ask students to focus their thinking on one of several areas:

- What do you *think* the answer to the question might be?
- What resources do you *think* we need to access to find answer to the questions?
- Whose perspectives do you *think* we are missing in our questions?
- What questions do you *think* we should focus on and why?
- What do you *think* about the primary source after visiting a secondary source?
- What do you *think* about the questions asked after visiting a secondary source?

Depending on the type of questions students ask and the next learning steps that a teacher wants students to take after the See, Wonder, Think strategy, he or she may focus the thinking task in one of several different areas. To push students' thinking in enhancing questions they have already asked, a teacher may ask students to continue working with questions. This may be done by identifying questions as closed- or open-ended or thick and thin questions. Students may then restate the question to change it from one type of question to another. A teacher may want students to narrow down their focus for research. He or she may ask students to select a set of questions and justify how answering those will work toward a learning goal. If prediction based on evidence and prior knowledge is of interest, the teacher may ask students to predict answers to questions. This may also be helpful if the focus is on recognizing the importance of finding reliable sources to support thinking. To focus on the information that will be accessed to answer the student questions, students may use the *Thinking* element of analysis to identify what type of resources they think they will need to answer the question or list locations where they think they will find the information.

Students may want to volunteer a new question or a revised version of a question while working on the last stage of See, Wonder, Think. As was mentioned earlier, there is always time to ask new questions. Celebrate that students continue to be thinking about questions and feel safe enough in the space to continue to offer them to the group.

In our working example, with the young students, the teacher may decide to use an additional strategy, to give students information and then revisit the question. By sharing bibliographic information, the teacher can give students information that will encourage them to revisit their questions.

You have come up of a lot of questions. Like any time we ask questions, sometimes we will be able to answer a question and sometimes we will not. To try to answer a question, we want to find a source of information. There was some information that came with this photograph and I think sharing that might help answer some questions. The person who took the photo gave it a title. Let's look at it and see what we can learn.

The title reads: "Seven-year-old Alex Reiber topping. He said, 'I hooked me knee with the beet-knife, but I jest went on a-workin'.' Location: Sterling [vicinity], Colorado / Photo by Hine, Oct 23/15."

Regardless of the age of elementary students, there are elements here that the teacher will want to consider before sharing with them. First, there is language that will likely be unknown, including the words "topping" and "beet-knife." Depending on time, the teacher may want to model how to find the meaning of those words or may simply want to have a word bank with definitions that are given with the photo title.

Just as the teacher made predictions about what questions the students would ask, he or she should also predict what information students will take from this title and what questions that may help answer. From this title, students can determine the following:

- The name of the boy in the photo
- How old the boy in the photo is
- What he was holding in his right hand
- The state where the photo was taken
- The time of year the photo was taken

Students may also surmise that the boy is holding a beet since he has a beet-knife and may guess that the photo was taken in 1915 given the unusual way the date is displayed.

You have learned some new information by reading this title. You also have definitions to two words, *topping* and *beet-knife*, that may help you understand this photo a little better. When you learn new information, it may help you answer some of your questions. Let's revisit your questions and see if we can answer any of them.

Make a point of letting students identify questions that have been answered and what the answer is. If there is no consensus, ask students to provide evidence to support their answer. As students finish identifying answers to questions, a teacher may challenge them to revisit their questions in a new way.

I like how you have used your new learning to help you answer your questions. Look at the questions we still have not answered. Take a look at the questions that you were able to answer. Now look at the title where you found the answers to the questions.

There is information in this title just like there was information in the photo. I'm wondering if learning about new information also made you wonder about new questions or want to change a question you or someone asked earlier. Take a moment to look at the questions and the new information. If you have a new question, let's add it to our list.

Some may be thinking that there could be no end to the number of questions that students could come up with if they continue to answer their own questions. That is true. Of course we have restrictions to our time, but with many elementary schools implementing a time for student independent exploration, independent reading, or nightly reading at home, there may be ways that this process of generating questions and answering them while generating new questions could segue

Exploring new images and bibliographic information related to the source may help students answer questions.

[Nine year old Mollie Keller and her two sisters, 10 and 13 yrs old, pulling beets. The overalls are used by many girls and women. They said they begin sometimes at 5 A.M., usually about 6 or 7, -and work until 6 P.M. with an hour off at noon. An 8 yr old sister works some. These 4 children, with the father and mother, work a large plot of beets on contract for W.E. Damm, near Sterling Colo. Mr. Damm said this family would make from $800 to $900 this season, with two or three hundred dollars out for expenses] Location: [Sterling vicinity, Colorado] / [Photo by Hine. Oct. 21/15]

into an opportunity for independent learning for those who are interested and motivated.

For these students, there are likely more questions. They may include the following questions:

- Who is Hine that took the photo?
- Was Alex all right after hurting himself with the knife?
- Why didn't Alex get help?
- Why was Alex cutting these beets in the field without any help?
- If this was taken in October, why wasn't Alex in school?
- Where is Sterling, Colorado?
- Why did children do this kind of work then when they don't do it now?

Remember that the scope of the questions will continue to rely on that student's personal experiences, but as that student is exposed to new information and encouraged to answer his or her own questions following the primary source analysis, that scope will be broadened, and the questions will reflect that.

Teacher's Role in the See, Wonder, Think Strategy

The teacher's role in the See, Wonder, Think strategy challenges that teacher to be nimble. He or she has to anticipate students' actions but be ready for the unexpected. Then the teacher must determine how to connect that unexpected response to future learning.

Teacher Roles Often Taken On

Like other strategies, in the See, Wonder, Think strategy, the teacher takes on the role of a facilitator. Focusing on students asking their own questions encourages a teacher to take on a specific role that will allow students to take charge of this element of their learning. As teacher takes on the role of a facilitator, he or she will always do the following:

- Select the appropriate strategy for students to formulate their own questions
- Choose the primary source focus for the analysis
- Decide on the type of collaboration that will take place during analysis

As mentioned earlier, students also generate questions in See, Think, Wonder. It is also likely that they are introduced to this strategy before See, Wonder, Think. There may be times when the teacher decides that See, Think, Wonder does a satisfactory job in helping students form questions. Other factors he or she may consider are time available, format of the primary source, and how the primary source analysis leads to other learning. These elements can be decided by a final consideration of how this primary source analysis will play out under the two strategies. That can be determined when the teacher imagines how the students would react to the primary source under the two analysis strategies. Ultimately, there is no wrong answer, only a preferred one. They are both beneficial strategies for students voicing questions about a primary source.

Depending on how strongly a teacher feels about a primary-source-analysis strategy compared to the primary source itself, the choice of the source is another factor to be considered. As mentioned earlier, there are aspects that may guide the decision. All of those, ultimately, revolve around how the primary source lends itself to help students write their own questions to lead to new learning.

The final decision that the teacher will always make is the type of collaboration among students during the primary source analysis. As suggested earlier, if students are new to the strategy, whole-class collaborative analysis is suggested, but older elementary students may move to working in small groups or pairs as they become more familiar with the strategy. It is mentioned specifically here because of the number of questions generated and written down during the analysis. The teacher may form collaborative groups of any size to maximize the student participation and number of questions generated while considering the time to consolidate, share, or have others react to students' questions when they are written in smaller groups.

Teacher Roles to Avoid Taking On

While there are key roles to be played as a facilitator of these two strategies for a classroom teacher, there are also roles to be avoided. Doing so gives ownership of the questions and the learning to students. They include:

- Judging, elevating, or negating questions
- Taking on the role of the secondary source to answer questions

In the See, Wonder, Think strategy, the goal is for students to generate as many questions as possible. Students may also evaluate those questions and narrow down their selection, but to do this effectively, they must have as many questions as possible related to the primary source and topic to choose from. If, during that process, the teacher judges the questions, this can inhibit students from asking more questions. This may cause them to prioritize what they believe the teacher wants in a question above the process of creating a large number of questions in the time given. Judging questions can be done by elevating a question, leaving other students to believe that other questions should, in some way, be like the one that the teacher approves of. The other way, of course, diminishes a question, suggesting that students should avoid questions like it.

Instead of evaluating student questions, either give information at the onset of the primary source analysis to hinder them from asking related questions or frame the task in a way that encourages others to be asked. As an example, in the analysis with the boy in the field, telling students that we are comparing their lives to lives of children from a century ago encourages comparative questions from today and long ago. This directly connects to the unit of study and provides a segue to future exploration while still empowering students to ask questions.

As questions are voiced by students, there will be times when there is no source available to that student to answer their question. While the teacher can be a partner or guide as students seek out information, he or she should avoid becoming the source or interpreter of information to answer questions that come from the primary source analysis. The overall concern is that discovery is taken out of the hands of the student and focused on the teacher. This sometimes happens for well-intended reasons. Sometimes, the teacher has knowledge that is more quickly shared than finding other sources. Other times, sources available are too complex or written in a way that may be difficult for an elementary student to understand. Maybe there is simply an excitement on the teacher's part that the student has independently asked a question that is also of interest to the teacher. In any case, as students transition from primary source analysis to other learning, keeping the focus of learning on their own discovery process is important.

Teacher Roles Sometimes Taken On

There are other tasks that a teacher may sometimes take on during the primary source analysis. Because of time, the students' familiarity with the strategy, or collaborative elements, the teacher may sometimes choose to step into a role to facilitate the analysis. He or she may be found:

- Recording students' questions
- Helping transition through stages during analysis
- Modeling formulation of a question or step in the process

Depending on the size of the group, a teacher may find himself or herself recording students' questions during the See, Wonder, Think strategy. When this strategy is done in a whole-class setting, it may make sense for the teacher to document student observations and questions to allow students to share ideas and questions more quickly. Students who write more slowly may also benefit from the teacher recording questions during a fast-paced primary source analysis.

The steps in these strategies can be difficult for some students to transition through independently, especially when they are new to the strategy and its structured stages. A teacher helping with transitions can help students move between tasks with more ease. This may mean not only announcing the time to transition but also previewing the new task and focus. The teacher may also bridge the transition by telling students how their earlier thinking will help as they move into the next step of analysis.

Lastly, during the primary source analysis, a teacher may want to model how he or she creates his or her own question. This may take the form of a think aloud as the teacher identifies an element in a primary source, connects it to some prior knowledge, and then relates the observation and idea to a question. The teacher may also demonstrate altering basic questions beginning with *who*, *what*, or *where* into more complex questions beginning with *how* or *why*. A teacher may also model prioritizing questions or any other extension to the strategy. The important thing to keep in mind is to not make this modeling permanent so that students can begin to practice and internalize the skills in the analysis strategies after seeing the teacher modeling.

Differentiating the See, Wonder, Think Strategy for Youngest Learners

Younger learners can perform this strategy at an early age even before working through the See, Think, Wonder strategy. There are some considerations that may make the analysis more successful in preparation. Teachers will want to consider the format of the primary source being used, likely focusing on a visual source with little or no text. This could include still images or videos. In the case of videos, silent film eliminates the need to process two mediums. Visual and sound not being interpreted together may be more easily analyzed to create questions by the youngest learners. In addition, the primary source should contain more obvious connections for younger students to relate to as well as clearly visible unknown elements for students to develop their questions around. These may become more complex as younger students increase their background knowledge throughout the year. A teacher will want to predict students going through the analysis process in the selection of the primary source to help predict how the source will impact the analysis.

During the analysis, as in the examples, the teacher will likely want to document student questions and other work to keep a faster pace to the primary source analysis and to more easily include emerging writers in the activity. This may require that primary source analysis is done collaboratively as an entire class or as a group as part of a rotation that the teacher is directly involved in.

Finally, a teacher will want to tailor his or her expectations regarding the depth of the questions. While our youngest students will surprise us with unexpected questions, a teacher should not expect the same sophistication in questions that would be expected from an upper-elementary student. Challenging students to write questions beginning with *why* and *how* can lead to more sophisticated questions. A teacher can make this a part of the introduction of the strategy so that students see this as part of the process and not a reaction to the questions they already formed.

Strategy 4: Analyzing Like a Historian Strategy

This strategy is modeled after Stanford History Education Group's Reading Like a Historian strategy where students focus on historical reading skills to make meaning from a primary source. This four-step process can be complex and is likely one a teacher would use after students are familiar with other primary-source-analysis strategies. The layers of analysis do encourage students to look at a piece from several different angles and give them a unique way to independently think about the primary source.

Strategy Overview

The Analyzing Like a Historian strategy guides students through a four-step process to analyze a primary source. The first two, sourcing and contextualizing, ask students to quickly identify basic information in the primary source and then place that source in a historical context. As students begin to carefully look at the source, they use a close reading or other analysis strategy to draw specific meaning from the source. Finally, students are asked to corroborate their understanding from this primary source with another primary source or other learning that has previously taken place.

Framing the Analyzing Like a Historian Strategy for Students

Like the name, Analyzing Like a Historian strategy encourages students to go beyond a basic analysis and bring in additional elements that historians often consider when viewing historical artifacts and documents. As upper-elementary students add these elements to their skill set, the idea that they are asking some of the same questions that historians ask on a regular basis should not be dismissed. Instead, introducing this strategy is an opportunity to point out the other primary-source-analysis strategies that the students are already familiar with, and equating their thinking with those of experts encourages students to continue to take ownership of their learning.

Students should know that the first time they use the Analyzing Like a Historian strategy, some of what they do will be familiar. Other parts of the analysis will encourage them to find and think about information that their teacher sometimes gave them or sometimes was not thought about at all.

For an illustrative example, we will look at an article and diary entry dealing with the shirtwaist makers' strike in 1909 (Figures 2.6 and 2.7). These may be used in an upper-elementary grade as illustrative pieces on a unit dealing with social justice or activism, possibly related to a piece of literature with the same overall focus. The primary sources give perspectives on the strike and the individuals taking part and impacted by it. It should be assumed that students have done some type of primary source analysis prior to the first time they use the Analyzing Like a Historian strategy.

We have been talking and reading lately about moments in history when actions by groups of people bring about some type of change. When we talk

Figure 2.6
December 6, 1909, *New-York Tribune*.

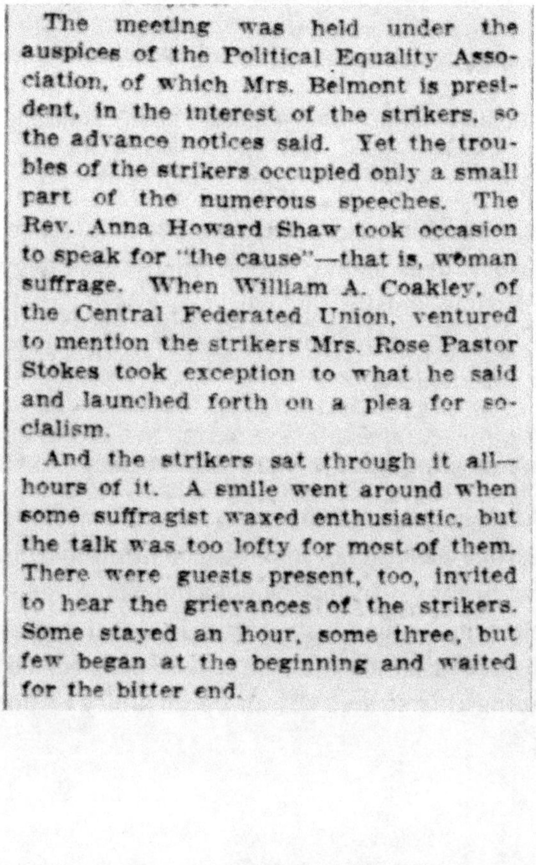

The meeting was held under the auspices of the Political Equality Association, of which Mrs. Belmont is president, in the interest of the strikers, so the advance notices said. Yet the troubles of the strikers occupied only a small part of the numerous speeches. The Rev. Anna Howard Shaw took occasion to speak for "the cause"—that is, woman suffrage. When William A. Coakley, of the Central Federated Union, ventured to mention the strikers Mrs. Rose Pastor Stokes took exception to what he said and launched forth on a plea for socialism.

And the strikers sat through it all—hours of it. A smile went around when some suffragist waxed enthusiastic, but the talk was too lofty for most of them. There were guests present, too, invited to hear the grievances of the strikers. Some stayed an hour, some three, but few began at the beginning and waited for the bitter end.

about a group of people though, we should keep in mind that the group is made of individuals and that those individuals aren't all identical.

Today, we're going to look at a set of primary sources around the shirt-waist makers' strike, one of the moments in history that we have talked about. We will use a strategy that builds on some of the primary source analysis work that you have already done.

To prepare to look closely at the sources, we are going to get our minds in a place where we can read and understand these sources and make the most sense from them. This is something that historians, people who study historical documents regularly, do all of the time. It helps them focus on the document, the event, and the time period. Then we will use a primary source analysis strategy that we have done many times. That will feel very familiar to you. Finally, you will compare your sources to each other to see what information matches between the two primary sources.

Two important things happen as the analysis is introduced. First, students are given some specific context around the primary source analysis. This is important because the teacher will ask them to activate that prior knowledge as part of the analysis itself. Reminding students while framing the analysis can spark some connections to prior learning. Second, the Analyzing Like a Historian strategy is overviewed, giving students some insight into the steps. While this is not always done as part of the framing, as students are familiarizing themselves with this strategy, providing an overview, while also pointing out that there are parts of what they will be doing that they are already familiar with, can help some students who may find the strategy complex.

Guiding Students through the Analyzing Like a Historian Strategy

The Analyzing Like a Historian strategy builds upon other primary-source-analysis strategies, emphasizing thinking skills that prepare students to analyze a primary source and then additional thinking to confirm thinking from a primary source analysis by corroborating the information with another source. This may be best done with the See, Think, Wonder Strategy or the Close Reading strategy, but others can be used as well.

In our framing of the strategy, we focused on the 1909 shirtwaist makers' strike. Students will read two related primary sources, a diary entry and a newspaper article, both related to a rally that was held in support of the strike and in conjunction with the women's suffrage movement. In this case, students have some familiarity with the time period because of picture books they have read, including *Brave Girl*, a picture book about Clara Lemlich, a woman who was a leader in the strike.

Guiding Students through Sourcing

After the teacher frames the primary source analysis with students, he or she guides them to the first of two initial stages of the analysis: sourcing. When sourcing, students find basic information about the particular primary source that they will apply to their analysis of the item. To do this, students are given both the primary source and any bibliographic data available on the source.

Bibliographic data, depending on how much is available, can be overwhelming, and not all of them are useful at this phase of analysis for these students. Nevertheless, quickly scanning a document for specific information is a good skill to practice. Provide students the full bibliographic information unless the bibliographic data reveal something that the teacher is wanting students to wonder about during the analysis or discover on their own during some other learning. If wanting to hold some information back, print out the bibliographic data and delete them.

Sourcing is a quick process and should take only three to five minutes. During that time, students are looking for key pieces of information to inform them about the source that can help them interpret the information during the analysis. A teacher may model this step with students multiple times if the concept is new to them. Even once they are familiar with the step, their teacher may give them a short list to remind them of the information they are looking for. He or she may begin by asking them several questions:

- What format is the source?
- Who created the source?
- When was it created?
- Why would someone create a source like this?

The first question and last question are linked. Identifying the source allows a student to answer why someone creates that type of source. Notice that the student is not trying to identify why a person created this particular source. Instead, this is a general question. Why would someone write in a diary? Diary entries may be written to keep track of events or to write down information they do not want to share with others. Why do people make maps? Maybe a map is created to show others how a space is organized or laid out. Why do people write a news story? More than likely, it is written to inform people. There may be more than one answer to a question about why a person would create a certain format of primary source. Students may write down both. Sourcing is not about writing down an answer that will be checked off as right or wrong by the teacher. It is about using ideas about why a source was made to make sense of the source during analysis.

When students ask who created a particular primary source, a name may tell them very little unless it is a historical figure that they know well. A letter written by Abraham Lincoln allows students to connect with what type of person they

Figure 2.7
The Diary of a Shirtwaist Striker by Theresa Serber Malkiel.

> **DECEMBER 5.**—Lord! I never saw anything like it in my life—that Hippodrome meeting. The place was so crowded that I had trouble in getting in, though I did come rather early. But once I was in it was worth all the trouble of getting there. It did my heart good to see how happy every one of our girls looked. There, more than in any other place, I felt the kinship between all the girls and myself. It seemed to me that their joy was my joy, their sorrow my own. It seemed as if I had grown a pair of wings that lifted me nearer to heaven. I sang and laughed, and was happy like all the rest of them. For I felt as though I had been born anew and became a power. I knew that if I should happen to be hurt or abused all these thousands of men and women would stretch out their hands to lift me out of danger.
>
> It is really a wonderful feeling that comes over one when a body finds itself surrounded by thousands of people all assembled for the same purpose, breathing the same hopes and thinking the same thoughts—it's like an immense giant born for the purpose of doing justice to all.

believe Lincoln to be. Students are connecting the person who created the source with context around the time period. If the person is unknown to students, providing them a sentence or two about who the person was can help them start to connect to that context. Without it, the name remains meaningless and simply a box to check off while sourcing, which is not what students should be doing.

In our example, the diary entry comes from a book titled *The Diary of a Shirtwaist Striker: A Story of the Shirtwaist Makers' Strike in New York* by Theresa Serber Malkiel. The author will likely not be known by the students, but the title gives us information about her. She is a shirtwaist striker, and she lived in New York. The teacher may ask his or her students, knowing that a student will target the title of the book, "You probably do not know this person. I didn't before I read some of her diary. What do we know about her from the bibliographic information?"

After students share information from the title, he or she can then follow up, "We know that this author is a woman, a shirtwaist worker, and a striker. Given what we know about the event, what else may be true about her?" With background information, they may know about the event that can draw some general ideas about the author.

A teacher may be hesitant to allow students to speculate at this point in the analysis. Remember that the goal is to encourage students to connect to the primary source. This is done by them drawing upon their own knowledge of the event as they take ownership of their learning. As they draw on that knowledge, they are making reasonable predictions about the author. As they are reading the diary entry later in the analysis, those speculations will give them the grounding to ask themselves, "Does this part of the diary make sense? Does it match what I thought she would write? If not, why not?"

Finally, students identifying when an item was created helps to connect a specific event to a time period. Depending on the student's knowledge of a particular historical time period, the date may bring to mind other historical events that took place during the same time. A student may also think of technology at the time, clothing, lifestyle, or cultural aspects that are related to that time period. These connections help the student move into the next stage of Analyzing Like a Historian: contextualization.

As students move through those three to five minutes of sourcing, the teacher may want to use a question to transition: "Could this be a reliable source to help us in our learning about the shirtwaist makers' strike and the change that came about because of it?" While elementary students will typically have reliable sources chosen for them by their teachers, the check on whether a source is beneficial to the intended learning will be essential as students select their own primary sources in middle and high school.

Guiding Students through Contextualization

Contextualization simply encourages students to begin thinking about the context surrounding the primary source. The moment in history and the event or person tied to the source are areas that students can draw upon. Like sourcing, contextualization helps a student make more meaningful connections to the primary source during the analysis. To help students begin contextualizing, a teacher can remind students of prior learning. When contextualizing, students focus on the following questions:

- What is happening during this time period?
- What do I know about this event?
- What connections to my own learning can I make?

> After sourcing, I want you to take a few minutes to contextualize. When we contextualize, we connect the primary source to the context around it. You told me, from your sourcing, that this diary was written in 1909 in New York. What was happening at this moment in history? What do you know about the people or the place at this moment in time. What events are going on in New York or in the United States in the early 1900s?
>
> You also told me that this diary entry is about the shirtwaist makers' strike. We read a picture book about that event. What do you remember from that picture book that might help you understand the diary? What was happening at that time? Why was it happening? Where was it happening? Who was involved? Take about five minutes to write down as much as you can about the context of this primary source.

Like sourcing, contextualizing is a short process. Students should not seek out other sources to reacquaint themselves with the topic or time period during the Analyzing Like a Historian strategy although pairs or small groups of students may contextualize together to recall previous learning. Students should spend no more than five minutes writing about the context of the primary source. The teacher may give even less time if he or she knows that students have very limited context. Contextualizing a primary source is not like writing an essay or report. Students may create a bulleted list, diagram, or sketchnote if that is a preferred way for them to write down their thinking. Through contextualization, they want to bring memories of a topic to the surface to help them make connections during the analysis. Students should finish these first two activities feeling like they are building toward something, not dragging out a moment.

Notice that in the example mentioned earlier, I refer to a picture book when introducing the contextualization stage. First, if context is not apparent to a group of students or if contextualizing is new, a teacher may want to point out moments of learning that they can draw context from. This may mean referencing a story, video, article, or learning activity that is related to the same topic as the primary source. This may take some planning on the teacher's part. If most students have limited context or no context, the teacher may want to find a nonfiction picture book, video, or some other medium that can give students some overview of information related to the primary source. If this is not part of an in-depth study, doing this a day or two prior to the primary source analysis can give students an opportunity to think back on earlier learning.

If time permits, a teacher may want to have a quick check-in with his or her class at the end of these two initial steps. It serves two purposes. First, the teacher may get a better sense of the collective knowledge of the group. What did they notice in their quick scan of the primary source? What prior learning have they begun to draw from? Are there any misconceptions that have surfaced that may lead to confusion during the next stage of analysis? Second, the check-in may be a model for students who are struggling with what to do during the sourcing and contextualizing stages and may give other students insights they had not thought about or thought to verbalize. A teacher's questions can help students reconnect with prior learning, but so can a fellow student's sharing about that same learning. As students share, the teacher can encourage others to add to their sourcing or contextualizing if they feel that they have heard something valuable. Remember though that students spent, at most, 10 minutes in these first two stages and maybe as short as 5 minutes. This check-in should be just as fast paced. This is not an opportunity for a complete debrief. Take a scattered number of volunteers, acknowledge the great thinking that others want to share, and move on.

Guiding Students through Analyzing the Source

After sourcing and contextualizing, students are ready to begin the main part of the primary source analysis. The point of these two steps is to activate students' thinking about a primary source and the topic under study in the hopes of making more meaningful connections to the primary source. As students are beginning this process, that may not be apparent, especially if they are familiar with the core primary analysis strategies. The teacher may help students make the transition.

Now that you have sourced and contextualized our primary source, you are ready for an analysis. We are going to use the See, Think, Wonder strategy. I know you have used this strategy many times before. You are really experts at it. This time though, you have done a lot of work with the primary source to prepare yourself for the analysis. You have activated your brain.

As you make your observations, reactions, and wonderings on this diary entry, think about what you already know about the primary source, about who created it, and why it may have been made. How can that help you understand the primary source? Think about when the diary entry was made. What do you know about what was happening during that time period and the event that was taking place when this diary entry was written? How does that help you make sense of the primary source and ask deep questions connected to it?

See, Think, Wonder is not the only strategy that can be used when Analyzing Like a Historian strategy is used. Students may use Close Reading strategy, a variation of one of these strategies, or any primary-source-analysis strategy where

Students can use any other analysis strategy within the Analyzing Like a Historian strategy.

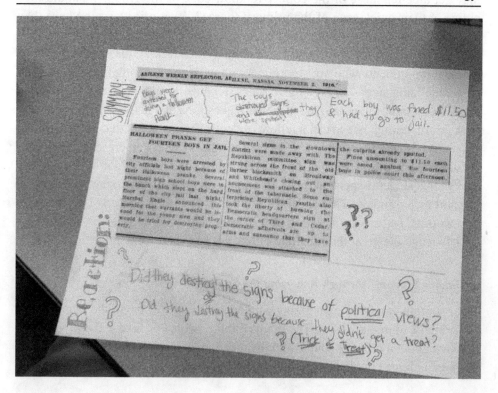

students look closely and react to a primary source. Look for evidence that students are using thinking from sourcing and contextualizing in their main analysis. Words or phrases from the initial stages may show themselves in a question or reaction to the primary source. A student may be more confident in his or her analysis, may write more, or may contribute more to a discussion after the analysis. If not seeing a benefit to sourcing and contextualizing, reflect on those teaching moments or talk to students to gain insights into how they are connecting them with the primary-source-analysis strategy.

After students analyze the primary source, there can be benefits to bringing additional sources into student learning. Not only can it help to provide more insight to add to a student's understanding of a topic but it also can confirm understandings of the event as they show themselves over multiple sources. To do this, students corroborate two or more sources.

In the example, a second primary source, a portion of a newspaper article, will be used. Students would again want to source the article to begin to understand when and why it was written. A teacher would also ask students to contextualize the article. Students may be resistant, explaining that they just contextualized a primary source on the same topic and time period. Encourage students to focus on what they just learned from their first primary source analysis in this contextualization. Because students are not writing as much context, the teacher may only give students five minutes total to source and contextualize the primary source. When analyzing, using the same strategy—in this case, the See, Think, Wonder strategy—keeps the students on a familiar path in this complex multistep process.

Guiding Students through Corroboration

After students have sourced, contextualized, and analyzed two or more primary sources, they are ready to corroborate the information. When students corroborate, they are looking for information that can be confirmed or information that builds upon information from another source. Finding information that connects gives it credibility, making it more likely to be true or believable. Information that builds can round out a moment in time, making the story of an event or a person more rich, multilayered, complex, and interesting.

As students begin to corroborate, the teacher may bring them back to the purpose for looking at the sources. Much like the Close Reading strategy, students may corroborate two or more sources through a lens to focus their attention on certain elements.

When we find connections between sources, they become more believable to us. In our own life, if one classmate told us about something that had happened on a day we were absent, we might trust what they say or we might not. But if several students shared their version of the same story, we can start to see what parts of their stories are being repeated and what parts connect. Even without being there, we get a clearer picture in our minds because we are comparing multiple sources and looking for these links. This is what we do when we corroborate primary sources.

As you begin to corroborate these two sources, think about the idea that groups of people can bring about change. Where is there evidence of change taking place? What does it look like? How do people in the two sources feel about the topic and the change around them? As you identify those in your sourcing, contextualization, and analysis, where are there relationships between the two sources? Where are there differences?

As with other primary source analysis, let students' connections surface. Students may work in pairs or groups to be able to talk through corroboration between documents. If a student struggles to find the relationships, the teacher may also want to look at a student's writing about a primary source. It is likely that the ideas to connect are there, but the student is having trouble drawing the line between them. When the teacher finds ideas between documents that may connect, ask a student to color-code a specific type of documentation within the analysis. In the example mentioned earlier, it may be ideas related to change. Then, revisit that limited number of items to look for similarities.

Corroboration can be challenging. The example deals with two text-based primary sources, but when different formats are used, students who have successfully corroborated two or more documents before may struggle to find the relationship between them. That does not mean that these pairings should be avoided. Descriptions of an event paired with a map or a photo can lead to powerful corroboration and learning. Instead, anticipate the possibility of students needing additional support through modeling or collaboration.

Teacher's Role in the Analyzing Like a Historian Strategy

The Analyzing Like a Historian strategy is complex because it is essentially an analysis strategy with another strategy embedded within it. This focuses the teacher's role on helping students transition through the Analyzing Like a Historian strategy and recognizing how to connect learning and thinking through the stages.

Teacher Roles Often Taken On

Through the Analyzing Like a Historian strategy, a teacher will find himself or herself doing the following:

- Selecting pairs or groups of primary sources that inform each other through corroboration

- Providing students bibliographic information to inform them about the primary source
- Focusing students' attention during different stages of analysis through prompts
- Being a timekeeper during the different stages of the analysis
- Guiding students in enhancing previously known analysis strategies by connecting thinking from new parts of the primary source analysis

It is not difficult to find primary sources that speak to the same topic. Identifying sources that also speak to each other can be more difficult. This is beneficial though as students corroborate information from the two sources. That is why selection becomes important. The primary sources must have something that connects them to corroborate but should not be carbon copies of each other. Maybe the sources have contrasting viewpoints. Possibly, they are from the same person but focus on different moments within an event. Two different formats, one visual and one written, encourage students to look for connections between the sources. Whatever the connections are, the teacher should be predicting when selecting the sources for his or her students.

As students source an item, they will need access to bibliographic information from the primary source. A teacher should not only provide or point students to that information but also encourage them to perform light research when there is more to be uncovered. If a quick search online will reveal that a person from history who created a primary source had a known perspective, that may be important to interpreting the source. These investigations should only take minutes. They are not meant to be a full inquiry, but modeling the investigation that a researcher would do encourages students to ask their own questions and go beyond just filling in a blank.

With a more complex primary-source-analysis strategy comes more time committed to it. A teacher should help students pace and transition through Analyzing Like a Historian strategy. This is certainly not a strategy to allow students to do independently. Reminding students of time, especially during sourcing and contextualizing, adds an importance to their immediate work. Transitioning to the Close Reading or See, Think, Wonder analysis by reminding them how their sourcing and contextualization can be applied gives purpose to the strategy as a whole. As a teacher guides students into corroboration, pointing out their level of expertise in what they just performed can give them confidence to use that expertise in the final stage of the Analyzing Like a Historian strategy.

Teacher Roles to Avoid Taking On

Like other analysis methods, there are roles that a teacher can take on that can hinder students' interactions with the primary source. These may include:

- Telling students why specific bibliographic information is important to a primary source prior to their analysis

- Providing students context on a source, topic, or time period as they are analyzing the primary source
- Performing elements of the primary source analysis that students have mastered to allow them to focus on new steps to the analysis

As mentioned, bibliographic information is key in students' sourcing an item during primary source analysis. It is important though that students are actually the ones sourcing the item. There will be times when a student may miss a key piece of information. Instead of telling them why the information is important, a teacher may choose one of two paths. He or she can remind the class about the areas that typically should be focused on when sourcing an item, encouraging them to ask specific questions or modeling possible questions to use if they are not sure why a piece of bibliographic information may be important. If that opportunity has passed, a teacher may briefly ask students to share out what they documented in their sourcing and why it may be important to the analysis. Neither of these guarantees that all students will focus on a specific piece of the bibliographic information, but if that one element is that important to the success of the entire process, there may be changes to the source, analysis strategy, or curriculum connection to be made.

Part of having connections to curriculum is students having some context when performing their primary source analysis. Students should arrive with that minimal context though and not be given it as part of the Analyzing Like a Historian strategy. There are already several stages and transitions for students to focus. If a teacher stops for a mini lesson to provide context, it can stop the momentum that students need. Instead, a teacher can provide context in a variety of ways prior to the primary source analysis.

These many stages and transitions in the Analyzing Like a Historian strategy take time. A teacher, when pushed for time, may think of only having students focus on parts of the strategy that are new to them. With other parts, such as a See, Think, Wonder within this larger strategy, there may be a temptation to provide students with analysis results instead of asking them to perform the analysis. Instead, a teacher may consider quickening the pace by allowing a shorter time for a strategy that students are familiar with, knowing that the thinking may not be as developed with less time to analyze a primary source. If the teacher recognizes that working in certain structures—for example, working in pairs—is most efficient for the students, he or she can group students to work more effectively. Finally, the teacher may choose a different primary-source-analysis strategy that fits within the time frame needed for students to adequately analyze the primary source with the time limitations that we all face in the classroom.

Teacher Roles Sometimes Taken On

Other roles may be taken on as students are learning the Analyzing Like a Historian Strategy or as needed because of other factors. These occasional roles include:

- Reminding students of a prior learning experience about a topic or time period related to a primary source
- Providing additional information about a creator of a primary source
- Providing organizational tools to help students display and connect their thinking during the analysis
- Encouraging students through the long analysis process by pointing out elements of the strategy they have already mastered
- Modeling elements of corroboration to assist students in making their own connections

Context is important and helping students connect prior learning to the Analyzing Like a Historian strategy can bridge a gap. A teacher may ask students to think about a previous lesson, discussion, or readings that he or she wants them to connect to the primary source analysis. This can happen as part of framing the analysis or as students are in the contextualizing stage of analysis. That context can extend to giving students additional information about the creator of the source or other information that can round out a student's understanding while sourcing a primary source. While students can do their own searches, a teacher may choose to provide the information to save time or model the questioning and searching process.

A teacher may also provide organizational tools such as graphic organizers or foldables to help students organize information. These organizational structures can help his or her students navigate the many steps of the Analyzing Like a Historian strategy and make connections between the thinking that is taking place during each stage. These tools may also embed streamlined versions of organizers from other analysis strategies. A teacher will want to be sure that references to previously mastered strategies are familiar enough that students will recognize them. These can provide a reassurance of the analysis process that they have already practiced.

Finally, a teacher may want to demonstrate the corroboration stage of the analysis process often. This complex stage may elude some students, and think alouds by the teacher can provide helpful modeling to guide students to more independent analysis. As more students begin to corroborate primary source documents successfully, a teacher may ask students to share their thinking or work in small groups to support those still striving to learn the skill.

Differentiating the Analyzing Like a Historian Strategy for Youngest Learners

Analyzing Like a Historian is a challenging strategy and one that an elementary school's youngest learners would likely not benefit from. This is because it builds upon other strategies already learned. Students may be in their last years of elementary school and have a good comfort level with other primary-source-analysis strategies before a teacher begins guiding his or her students through Analyzing Like a Historian strategy.

Instead of students performing this strategy, two important approaches can be taken with younger learners to prepare them for Analyzing Like a Historian strategy. First, give them many opportunities to perform a variety of different primary-source-analysis strategies. In addition, there are small elements of Analyzing Like a Historian strategy that can be incorporated into discussions about primary sources. There may be times when a teacher wants to show students bibliographic information and point out or have students find the creator of the work or when it was created. Other times, discussions about the creation date of a primary source and what was happening at the time may be a natural part of the learning. A teacher may read his or her students a picture book focused on a historical event or person to provide context before introducing them to a primary source for them to analyze. Young students may have the option of analyzing two primary sources related to one event. Brainstorming, as a group, what the connections are between those two sources can begin to lay the groundwork for corroboration in upper grades. So, while the analysis strategy itself may not be developmentally appropriate for an elementary school's youngest learners, adding elements of Analyzing Like a Historian strategy to other primary source analyses or on their own when interacting with primary sources can provide critical skills and learning opportunities.

A Special Note about the Analyzing Like a Historian Strategy

It was shared earlier, but it is worth sharing again. The Analyzing Like a Historian strategy is challenging and complex. This is why it is the only strategy that I suggest using in its entirety only with upper-elementary students. It is also a time commitment. The many steps and use of multiple sources, even when paced aggressively, add up to a large amount of class time. It may appear that this strategy is to be avoided at all costs, but there are times when it makes sense to consider the strategy or parts of it.

Like the suggestions for youngest learners, consider using parts of Analyzing Like a Historian strategy when they benefit another primary-source-analysis strategy. Are students already analyzing multiple primary sources? Corroborate as a class to find connections between their thinking. Using a new format of primary source with a group of students? Source the item so that students purposefully consider why people create those formats of primary sources. Want to be sure students are relating the primary source analysis to prior learning? Have them do a quick contextualization. As these parts of the process are incorporated regularly in student learning, embracing the full Analyzing Like a Historian strategy becomes less daunting.

The full Analyzing Like a Historian strategy may be used best as part of a larger research project that utilizes primary sources as part of the research process. Bringing the strategy in at this time encourages students to focus on the learning that can come from primary sources, especially when they are brought together with secondary sources during corroboration. That element of a primary source encouraging a student to wonder makes it a great part of the research process. Unlike a textbook, a website, or a nonfiction book, the primary source likely will not give the complete story. That missing piece of the story engages students in the mystery and encourages them to use analysis techniques to make meaning from, question, and interact with the primary source. They construct understanding through the analysis of primary sources and connect their analysis to prior knowledge and learning from secondary sources.

The layers of analysis that help students make deep meaning happen when sourcing and contextualizing can be a powerful part of the research process. The connection between primary sources and secondary sources comes through corroboration of multiple types of sources. Trying to introduce these skills during a research process would be ill advised. Instead, as suggested earlier, incorporate them into other primary-source-analysis opportunities, and students will become seasoned in the steps of the strategy.

Strategy 5: Using Visible Thinking Strategies as Exit Slips

Visible Thinking strategies encourage students to express their thinking through voice or writing. One notable resource is Harvard's Project Zero, which has a wealth of resources that encourage this type of sharing that makes thinking more evident and also helps students process and reflect on their own learning. This type of work pairs well with the deep levels of thinking that happen as students fully engage with a primary source. Elementary teachers can use variations of these strategies as a way to gain evidence of student thinking. This can help when reviewing the effectiveness of a lesson and help support future learning.

Strategies Overview

Visible Thinking strategies can be presented as an exit slip, a quick-written response from a student that gives the teacher insight into a student's learning. This may be submitted on a digit form or written on a slip of paper. The purpose is to get feedback that is quick for a student to produce and for a teacher to read and evaluate. These exit slips may be an observation of the class as a whole or may bring awareness about a single student. They typically are formative assessments that a teacher can apply to help bridge the learning from the primary source analysis to the connected learning.

There are many reasons why a teacher may want to use an exit slip with a Visible Thinking strategy at the end or at a pivotal point within a lesson. Possibly, the teacher only had time to focus on one part of a primary source analysis but wants a larger insight into how his or her students view the primary source. Maybe the teacher wants to try a new primary source analysis or a variation on the analysis. A Visible Thinking exit slip may help the teacher understand the impact of the strategy on student thinking. There may also be lessons where students perform a primary source analysis and the teacher's understanding of student learning is unclear. Any of these warrant a Visible Thinking strategy exit slip.

Framing the Visible Thinking Strategies for Students

Used as an exit slip, there is fairly minimal framing to the use of Visible Thinking strategies. Students will have already interacted with a primary source. They will have done one of the analyses in this book, a variation, or some other type of primary source analysis. At the point of bringing in the exit slip, students have had a substantial interaction with the primary source.

> As you finish up your primary source analysis, I'm going to give out an exit slip that I would like everyone to complete. This is going to give me an idea of how you connected with the primary source and how that impacted your thinking. There is not a single right answer here. The trick is that it is somewhat short. You will only write a couple sentences. That might tempt you to write something down without giving it much thought, but I know you have all been doing a lot of thinking today. Take a little time and make sure that shows through here.

There are two things that should be evident as a teacher frames a Visible Thinking exit slip. The first is the purpose for asking students to fill it out. Be sure that the intention is authentic and transparent to students. The second is that like any primary source analysis writing, there is not a right or wrong answer, but there is a correct approach. Here, the teacher warns students that the exit slip might look deceptively simple, but the goal is for students to represent the thinking they just did during the earlier primary source analysis. Any framing of a Visible Thinking exit slip should share the purpose and motivate students to share their thinking in a concise way.

Guiding Students through Visible Thinking Strategies

There are many ways that a teacher can gain insight into a student's thinking following a primary source analysis. These insights may revolve around the student's thinking about the topic under study. In this case, the following prompts or a varia-tion may be used:

- I used to think ... but now I think ...
- Now I think ... because ...
- I wonder ... I think ... (Here a student asks a question and answers his or her own question.)
- The text said ... and that connects to ... and that makes me believe ...

Other Visible Thinking prompts may give insights into a student's reflections on the author or creator of a primary source. The following prompts address these types of reflections:

- I think the author's purpose for writing this piece was ... because ...
- I think the author wants the reader to believe ... because ...
- I think the creator of the source wants the viewer to believe ... because ...

If the primary source analysis focuses on the original audience for the source, the following Visible Thinking prompts can show a student's understanding:

- I think the original audience for this source was ... because ...
- I think the original reader felt ... after reading the text because ...
- I think the original audience felt ... after seeing this because ...

Some Visible Thinking prompts ask a student to focus on one element of his or her primary source analysis. This may give insight into what the student found most important, was most engaged by, or may be most interested in exploring in future learning. These exit slips include:

- I noticed ... and that made me think ...
- I noticed ... and that made me wonder ...
- Something new ... My connection to it ... My question about it ...
- I saw ... and that makes me want to learn more about ...

What can be seen here is that Visible Thinking exit slips, just as much as any primary-source-analysis strategy, should have a purpose. What a teacher wants to know from his or her students guides what exit slip is chosen and paired with the earlier experiences with the primary source.

Examples of Exit Slips in Use

Let's look back at the primary source analyses discussed earlier in this chapter and explore how a Visible Thinking exit slip may be used in conjunction with the main primary source analysis.

Exit slips may be anonymous if the teacher just wants an overall reaction to the primary source analysis.

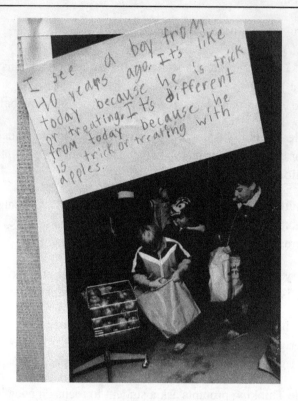

One group of students analyzed a photo of the Statue of Liberty using the See, Think, Wonder strategy in a larger study of American symbols. The teacher has several secondary sources connected to this same topic. Before the teacher chooses one, he or she wants to know what the students are interested in learning more about. The teacher chooses the *I saw ... and that makes me want to learn more about ...* Visible Thinking exit slip.

> There were many great questions that you posed as you analyzed this photo of the Statue of Liberty. Tomorrow, you will have a chance to explore more about the statue. There is a lot of interesting history about the statue, but I'm curious what you want to know more about. In your visible thinking exit slip I want you to take moment to think about what you want to explore more tomorrow. I also want you to think about the photo that you analyzed and what in the photo connects to what you want to know more about.
>
> I'll read over everyone's exit slips tonight. Tomorrow we'll have other resources that you will be able to use to explore your question.

In another example, students looked at newspaper advertisements from the 1910s for chocolate and sweets. In an effort to look at messaging in advertising, they used the Close Reading strategy to examine word choice within the text. As a final look at student understanding of the impact of word choice, a teacher may select the *I think the creator of the sources wants the viewer to believe ... because ...* Visible Thinking exit slip.

> You have analyzed several advertisements today, but we want to do more than just study them, we want to look for an overall message that came from the people who created these advertisements. We know what they wrote, but why did they write it? What did they want the people who read those advertisements to believe? The exit slip gives you an opportunity to share your thinking.

If this element had been addressed in the Close Reading strategy, the teacher may decide to use the Visible Thinking exit slip as an extension to the initial primary source analysis. Using the *I think the original audience for this source was ... because ...* exit slip in this instance encourages students to connect the message to an intended audience. In this case, there is strong evidence that the audience for these candy and chocolate advertisements is parents, likely one that most students may not initially suspect.

In the See, Wonder, Think analysis strategy example, students viewed a Lewis Hine photo of a boy on a sugar beet farm. The young students analyzed the photo to compare life now to life then. Since the focus of the primary-source-analysis strategy is to question, the teacher selects a Visible Thinking exit slip that encourages students to voice a question: the *I noticed ... and that made me wonder ...* exit slip.

> You've had a chance to look at just one boy that lived a hundred years ago. There are so many more people that we will learn about. These people lived different lives and we will get a chance to learn more about them. For today, think back to one thing that you noticed either in the photo or the description of the photo, one thing that you won't forget. Think about what that was and also what it makes you wonder about. It might make you wonder something about the boy or his parents, the person taking the photo, or someone else. Maybe it made you wonder about other children from one hundred years ago. In your exit slip today, write down one thing you saw and what it made you wonder about.

Finally, in the Analyzing Like a Historian strategy, students compared, analyzed, and corroborated two accounts of a rally connected to the shirtwaist makers' strike. Looking through a lens of working toward change, students explored a firsthand account of a woman who was striking during the 1909 event. Anticipating that ideas students have around those who strike or sacrifice for change have been altered after the primary source analysis, the teacher uses the *I used to think . . . but now I think . . .* Visible Thinking exit slip.

> You have had a chance to see a firsthand account of a woman who was striking during the shirtwaist makers' strike as well as a newspaper account of the same event that she attended. While she is just one person, she may challenge your idea of someone who takes part in an activity like this. Take what you thought about the event before analyzing the primary sources and compare it to what you think now. Share those thoughts in the exit slip.

Visible Thinking exit slips can be used in conjunction with another primary source analysis to extend thinking or to give every student an opportunity to voice an idea, reaction, or wondering about a primary source. They can gauge understanding, assist a teacher in making choices about connected learning, and provide evidence of students' levels of engagement with the primary source.

Teacher's Role in Visible Thinking Strategies

These interactions between teacher and student, although brief, are important because they are an opportunity for the teacher to gain insight about a student's perception of the primary source analysis.

Teacher Roles Often Taken On

There are several elements that a teacher will want to be sure to put in place every time a Visible Thinking exit slip is used. They include:

- Being transparent about purpose
- Choosing a Visible Thinking exit slip that will give insights being looked for
- Using findings as formative information
- Following up with students about new insights into their learning

Visible Thinking exit slips connected with students interacting with primary sources need to have a purpose. That may sound obvious on its surface, but a teacher identifying the reason why a Visible Thinking exit slip is being given to students will help define what Visible Thinking strategy he or she wants students to interact with or modify to get a specific type of information from his or her students' reflections. The teacher knowing the purpose behind the Visible Thinking exit slip will also make it much more likely that he or she will not only read the students' thoughts but also use that to inform future learning. That might mean that the teacher will alter the instruction in future primary source analyses, choose to use a different strategy, or modify the primary source analysis in some way. Student feedback might immediately impact learning, leading learning connected to the primary source analysis in a different direction than the teacher originally anticipated. Not only can the teacher alter instruction on the basis of these responses but he or she should also share these insights with students. A teacher conferring with students about how their successes, struggles, or interests were seen in their words they shared is important. It builds relationships and trust and most importantly shows students that their work and reflection on their work are important.

Teacher Roles to Avoid Taking On

It would seem that using a Visible Thinking strategy in a small moment at the end of a learning experience would be simple. In many ways it is, but there are types of exit slips that may not be Visible Thinking strategies and may not serve the teacher or students well. A teacher should avoid:

- Giving an exit slip that doesn't allow students to show their learning
- Giving an exit slip with no purpose to benefit future student learning
- Giving an exit slip where students have to write more than a few sentences

A teacher may want to alter a Visible Thinking strategy to meet his or her needs. He or she should be sure that the alteration continues to ask students to make their thinking visible. If students are asked about their enjoyment of an activity or prompting them to check boxes next to preselected reactions, the exit slip has moved away from being a Visible Thinking strategy. These do not ask them to reflect on their own learning in a meaningful way. On the other end of the spectrum, these Visible Thinking strategies are meant to be short. Students should not be writing a paragraph, asking for more paper, or taking large amounts of time to write their response. Visible Thinking asks students to reflect on their thinking, not give a full account of it. It is also much less likely that a teacher will have time to read these longer reactions and use them in a formative way.

Teacher Roles Sometimes Taken On

There can occasionally be additional benefits to using Visible Thinking strategies in an exit slip. These may prompt a teacher to find himself or herself:

- Using information from Visible Thinking to give students choice to bridge to new learning
- Following up with individual students to address student frustrations or misconceptions

Asking students to share their reflections in a Visible Thinking exit slip encourages a teacher to be nimble. Primary source analysis gives ownership of learning to students. This ownership may show itself as specific interests in a topic that was being studied during the analysis. If a teacher sees this, he or she may be able to alter instruction. This can help assure engagement and give students a powerful message about following their interests in their own learning.

Visible Thinking can also reveal misconceptions or frustrations as students struggle to voice their thinking. As students often work collaboratively during a primary source analysis, this may be the only time that a teacher is able to gain direct feedback from a student. These findings may prompt a one-on-one between teacher and student so that the teacher can address the misconception or frustration. This can benefit the student immediately as he or she takes understanding from the primary source analysis into new learning. The student will likely also find benefits by being more at ease the next time that primary-source-analysis strategy is used.

Differentiating Visible Thinking Strategies for Youngest Learners

Even young learners can provide feedback about their learning experiences. The teacher will still want to tell students why he or she is asking for their feedback and motivate them to share ideas about their thinking. Consider how the students can most easily reflect on their own learning and share that with the teacher.

The youngest elementary students may be beginning writers. Even writing a couple of sentences and expressing complex ideas about learning may be challenging. Consider letting these students think aloud with a partner and then share out as part of a class discussion. The teacher may want to make note of ideas students are sharing, documenting their thinking for them.

If the class has the capability, the teacher may ask students to make a short recording where they verbally respond to a prompt about an earlier primary-source-analysis activity. Since exit slips are meant to be short, the teacher may want to incorporate a timer into the student recording so that watching those remains manageable.

There are so many ways that students can interact with primary sources. These are just a few strategies that have benefited my students' learning and my teaching. Teachers should feel free to alter and modify these strategies and seek out new strategies for elementary students to analyze primary sources. As long as they keep in mind the core idea of students working together to take ownership of their own learning in a primary source analysis, they will likely create great opportunities for their students to learn from these incredible resources.

Chapter 3

Selecting Primary Sources

When I first brought primary sources into my students' learning, I used photos and drawings of events. The visual nature was appealing, and I thought I could pair them well with secondary source texts. Every time my students worked with these images, I paid close attention to how they reacted to them and how I reacted to my students. Many times, they were drawn in to tiny details. Sometimes they focused on things in the photo that I didn't think were important to what I wanted them to learn. I worked on my ability to frame the analysis so that students were still in charge of their learning, but I was helping to guide them. For a brief moment, I thought I had primary sources in student learning mastered.

Then my students started working with text-based primary sources. It only took me a moment to realize that changing formats changed how students interacted with a primary source. That also meant that I had to change how I approached my support. We worked with letters, newspaper articles, declarations, and diary entries. I brought in a note that was written in a cursive writing and, for a moment, all hope was lost. But as I continued working with different formats, I continued to realize how I could support my students.

Some of the last formats I used with students were audiovisual formats. Silent films, old television shows, and radio interviews were all opportunities to see how students would interact to different primary sources and what I could do to help them interact with the sources and analyze these primary sources to make meaning from them.

What format I was going to use was always one consideration, but overall, I wanted the primary source to be compelling, to draw students in. I considered what would engage them, how they would interact with it, and what about it made it the best choice from dozens or more possible choices.

Often, teachers will have an idea of using primary sources as a part of student learning, and they may think in terms of format. They may think, "I would love for my students to look at some old photos of what this area looked like in the past," or "I wonder if that person kept a diary. It would be so interesting to see their thinking." These are great starting points. Having an idea of what may be available can initiate a search, but try not to let formats limit the search. Historic photos can tell us one thing, but what type of learning can take place with maps from the same time period? Better yet, what if students had both? A diary may help a reader get inside the thinking of a historical figure, but what if that is not available? Would letters the person wrote be beneficial? What about letters written to that person or newspaper articles written about them?

Format is not the only consideration when selecting a primary source, but it is one that a teacher will want to acknowledge. The format gives clues about how students will interact with and learn from the primary source. That gives the teacher insights into how to support students in interacting with the source. It even helps a teacher estimate how long the analysis may take. All of this together makes format a key aspect to primary source analysis.

Choosing Compelling Primary Sources

It is important for teachers to put thought into the primary source that students will interact with. It impacts the analysis of the source and the connection with other learning (Figure 3.1). It is beneficial for a teacher to consider how his or her students will react to a primary source. That includes thinking about whether it will be engaging, but when searching for a primary source, there may be dozens or even hundreds of search results. Choosing one or two compelling primary sources can be a challenge because what makes a primary source compelling can be a variety of aspects.

Figure 3.1
Considerations Graphic.

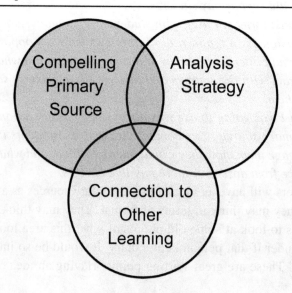

Some primary sources are compelling to students because of the following reasons:

- Students connect to the source.
- The source is well known or familiar.
- The source makes students wonder.
- The source is a particular format.
- The source elicits an emotional reaction.

A primary source ultimately should hold more than one of these characteristics to be truly compelling. Some of these even seem to be in contrast to each other. How can a primary source not only be familiar but also make a student wonder? A compelling primary source should be a combination of the familiar and the unknown. Format should be a consideration, and students should draw some connection to the source.

What Makes a Primary Source Compelling?

Connection

People are drawn to others because of connections. The same can be true of primary sources. The connections can be vast though, and there are many for a teacher to look for. Connections can be related to school. A teacher may find a source that students will connect with because of previous studies, the unit they are studying right now, or a piece of literature. There may also be a connection between the student and an individual focused on in the source. Age typically plays a part. Elementary students connect with primary sources that focus on children from the past. But the more that is revealed about the person in the source, the more opportunities there are for connections to be made. Connections could also be geographic. Finding primary sources from your state, city, or even neighborhood is an instant draw for students. Maps that depict these places from the past, even if they weren't made there, can also be a connection.

Well-Known or Familiar

Iconic primary sources can draw a person in. There is an instant familiarity. The process of analyzing that iconic primary source can then reveal previously unseen observations or new thinking. Students may also be drawn to primary sources created by well-known individuals. A letter from a popular president, a film, or a photo of a famous inventor can be enough to bring students to the piece and encourage them to begin their analysis.

Makes You Wonder

If students look at a primary source and instantly feel as if they know everything about it, they will likely feel like there is no reason to analyze the source. Instead, if there is some element that makes them wonder, they can be compelled to dig deeper. One way this can happen is that the primary source shows students something that is unexpected. Other sources may focus on historical figures or events that are well known but reveal flaws or unknown aspects to them. Keep in mind that these primary sources do not just show something students do not know, but it actually makes them want to know something about the person or event related to the primary source.

Format

Just the format itself can play a role in a primary source being compelling. This may happen in two ways. If students are familiar with using a particular format—for example, photographs—and also enjoy working with them, analyzing a primary source photograph can be a welcome task. Sometimes a completely new format may be what makes the primary source compelling. After working with visuals, moving to text-based or audiovisual primary sources can be a welcome change that will engage students.

Elicits an Emotion

One empowering aspect to primary source analysis is the ability for students to react to the source. One reaction that can be powerful is an emotional reaction to the source. When students feel an emotion when interacting with a source—anger, joy, or surprise—they connect with it. That emotional reaction can encourage students to continue interacting with the source. Not only will students remember the source but they also will remember the emotion connected with interacting with the source.

Let's look at a few Thanksgiving primary sources and explore what made them compelling choices for students to analyze.

In kindergarten, format and making connections were deciding factors. It was early in the year, and I knew I wanted an image. Any text would have to be read to them and too much would be a barrier. When choosing a photo titled *School Children's Thanksgiving Games, 11/27/11* (Figure 3.2), I was drawn to the fact that this was a group of elementary students in their school yard. For my students new to school, it would provide a connection that they could relate to. My young students would be preparing for a Thanksgiving celebration, so I knew they would have ideas about what may be happening in this photo.

With a fourth-grade class, familiar connections and focusing on a different format were strong considerations. I had wanted to continue an earlier focus on

Figure 3.2
School Children's Thanksgiving Games.

traditions, specifically food traditions. We had already looked at old newspaper advertisements for Thanksgiving foods, so I wanted to look at a different format. Many had expressed that one thing they had not seen in the advertisements we had looked at was Thanksgiving stuffing. That led to this cookbook from 1796. The recipe for stuffing was related to a previous discussion, so there was an element of connection (Figure 3.3). It was written with the long S, which can cause some students to have trouble reading it, but it also is short and contained

Figure 3.3
To Stuff a Turkey.

To ſtuff a Turkey.
Grate a wheat loaf, one quarter of a pound butter, one quarter of a pound ſalt pork, finely chopped, 2 eggs, a little ſweet marjoram, ſummer ſavory, parſley and ſage, pepper and ſalt (if the pork be not ſufficient,) fill the bird and ſew up.
The ſame will anſwer for all Wild Fowl.
Water Fowls require onions.
The ſame ingredients ſtuff a *leg of Veal, freſh Pork* or a *loin of Veal*.

mostly familiar ingredients. There is more about students reading historical documents with the long S later in this chapter.

Fifth-grade students analyzed a source that was chosen because I thought it would make them wonder. While students do not study the American Civil War, they are familiar with it. I thought a sketch titled *Thanksgiving in Camp Sketched Thursday 28th 1861* may make students wonder about Thanksgiving in a particular moment in time (Figure 3.4). The sketch clearly shows men in uniform in a camp with tents. Instead of what students may expect to see, men at war, there is a scene of celebration. Men are gathered at a table. Pots are over a fire. One soldier carries what may be a turkey and has a dog at his feet. The sketch takes two known events—the Civil War and a Thanksgiving celebration, two things that elementary students do not think of together—and places them at the same moment. I thought that idea of them seeing these two events together would make them wonder.

Notice that a teacher has to know his or her students, their curriculum, and experiences when selecting compelling primary sources. There are other elements that make the analysis successful such as the analysis strategy and how the primary source analysis is framed, but selecting a compelling source is a key factor in a successful primary source analysis.

Figure 3.4
Thanksgiving in Camp Sketched Thursday 28th 1861.

Analyzing Primary Source Images

Images may be the first types of primary sources that many elementary students work with. They can be used with any age student with reading not being a necessary skill to interact with the source. Students have the opportunity to bring in their visual literacy skills, and they often feel, even in a drawing, that they are seeing an actual moment, something that does not always come across in text.

Types of Primary Source Images

There are many different types of primary source images that students can use (see Table 3.1). Choosing one often is determined not only by what a teacher wants students to see but also by what is available that was created at that time period for that topic under study.

Considerations When Selecting Primary Source Images

Images add a visual appeal to any lesson, but what do teachers need to think about when selecting primary source images to incorporate into student learning through primary source analysis?

Portraits, Drawings, Sketches, and Engravings

Teachers may look at sources like artistic portraits or sketches and think that they cannot be primary sources because they are artistic interpretations of a person or event. I would disagree. While they are indeed an interpretation, one could easily describe a map as an interpretation. This is evident by the number of maps from the time of exploration in North and South America that have incorrect elements in them. Cartoons and political cartoons, while not always considered as artistic as a painted portrait, are artistic in nature. Even photographs are taken by a photographer who is making a decision to point the camera and capture one scene and not another.

Table 3.1
Types of Primary Source Images

Photos
Drawings, sketches, or engravings
Portraits
Cartoons
Political cartoons
Advertisements
Posters
Maps

The point is that there is interpretation, perspective, and even bias in every primary source students will encounter. There will be times that a teacher will want to help students discover that through their analysis. To return to the idea of an artistic piece as a primary source, if created at the time of the topic under study, it is one person's interpretation of that event. Equally interesting is that if the work was shared widely, that artistic print influenced what people at the time thought of an individual or event depicted. These are perfect reasons to consider these primary sources not only artistically but also historically.

A teacher may look to specific elements when selecting these artistically influenced visual primary sources. For drawings, sketches, or engravings, he or she can look at what will attract students' attention. How is color or style used to influence how the students will interpret the person or event in the piece?

In a portrait, a teacher can look for visual elements beyond the person. What other items accompany the individual? What can inform the student about the person in the portrait? What about the background, how is the person posed, or what is the person wearing? While a traditional headshot of an individual may show students what that historical figure looked like, it will likely not tell them much else about that person when it lacks other features.

Text in Primary Source Images

Some of these types of images likely have accompanying text. Cartoons and political cartoons likely have text boxes or word bubbles. Visual advertisements can be heavily illustrated and have small amounts of text. Maps will have labels, map keys, and titles. Even an old photograph can have its title or date scratched into the negative. A teacher may think about how students will interact with the text elements of a mainly visual primary source.

A teacher will want to consider the vocabulary for any text in the primary source image. Words and phrases that distract from the focus of the analysis may cause a teacher to not select that particular primary source. If the source is too compelling, vocabulary support may need to be prepared by the teacher prior to the analysis. The mystery vocabulary could actually be the focus of the analysis as well. Students may be challenged to determine the meaning of the word on the basis of the visual elements accompanying it.

It is not unusual for even an elementary student who is more experienced in primary source analysis to overlook text in these situations. Maybe other elements of the photo become so engaging that they do not notice the text. Whatever the reason, a teacher should decide if the text is critical to understanding the visual primary source and the additional learning that is to follow. If not, the teacher may not be concerned about students focusing only on the visuals. If the text is important, he or she will want to look for evidence that students are incorporating analysis of the text into their primary source analysis.

Students benefit from an up close look at a printed primary source image.

Student Interactions with Primary Source Images

Determining How Students Will Interact with the Source

After selecting the primary source, the teacher will want to determine how students will interact with the image. Typically there are three options. Students may interact with a print, a projection, or a digital image. Often, elementary students can benefit from interacting with a source in multiple ways throughout the analysis, leading the teacher to select more than one option.

Students of all ages can benefit from being able to have their own printed copy of a primary source image. Before the analysis, students may touch the image, tracing outlines or imagining texture. During the analysis itself, students often like to annotate directly onto the image. This may be circling things they observe, writing an idea or question in the margin, or drawing arrows. All of these give physical evidence of their thinking and put them more directly in touch with the primary source.

Many primary source images are in color though, and color printing can be costly. If it is possible to print the class a set of color prints, the teacher may not want them drawn on and only used once. Slipping the printed primary source image into a clear page protector can be an alternative. Some work well with dry erase markers and can allow students to do some of their annotating on the image. Because the quality of printing varies, teachers should print a test copy, even if printing in black and white. Certain printers and copy machines can cause details to fade that may be important to students making observations during a primary source analysis.

Projecting a primary source image also can benefit students' analysis, especially when the teacher wants to focus on a whole-class collaborative discussion. A class can see an image together. One student describing an observation can physically point to what he or she sees, avoiding the delay of others searching on individual papers as they work to remain part of the discussion. If used with an interactive whiteboard, digital projections can also document analysis, holding text and annotations to be returned to later by saving the file. Digital projection also gives the teacher an opportunity to zoom in on a portion of the primary source image to focus on an area. This can be especially helpful when there is a question about what the image shows or there are fine details to be seen. Of course, the resolution of the digital image and the software being used to show the image should support this type of zoom-in to take advantage of this benefit to projecting the image.

There are technical considerations to project a primary source image. Similar to print, if the color of the print is important to the analysis, the teacher will want to be sure that the projector shows true color. Darkening rooms can help overcome projections that are not as crisp as images shown on a computer screen.

The final way that elementary students may interact with the primary source is by looking at a screen on a desktop, laptop, or handheld device. Regardless of the type of device, students benefit from a two-to-one or one-to-one environment when viewing a primary source image in this way. Like students having their own print copy, students may get extremely close to the screen to see details or touch the screen as they investigate a source. Students who are sharing a device will instantly have a partner to discuss the image, share observations, and move through the prescribed analysis together.

Using devices that allow students to control zooming in on the image is a way to put students in control of their own analysis. Clicking or pinching on a spot in an image to pull forward more detail allows a class of students to each be investigating a different element of the primary source simultaneously. This ability to zoom in to see more detail works especially well with primary source maps. Other software that allows students to type or annotate directly on a digital image gives another way to enhance the engagement of students during analysis. Upper-elementary students may be comfortable toggling between a primary source image and a document to record their analysis. These students may also take advantage of shared documents online where students can collectively record their observations, ideas, and questions as part of the analysis.

Students can zoom in on fine details when viewing a primary source on a screen.

There is not one right answer to how students should interact with a primary source image during an analysis. A teacher may choose to have students start with print images and then transition to a projected image. Students may begin looking at the image together on an interactive whiteboard and move to pairs of students sharing a mobile device to look more closely while still having a collaboration partner. The point is to match the print, projection, or digital with the desired interaction a student will have both with the primary source image and with peers.

Modified Analysis for Primary Source Images

Analyzing a primary source image can lend itself to modifying or specializing the type of analysis. These few examples are not exhaustive. As a teacher sees suggestions on how students can be visually literate, he or she can ask how the same suggestions would impact a primary source analysis. These may take the form of their own analysis strategy or may be used to modify an existing strategy.

The See, Think, Wonder strategy works well with any format of primary source. When working with primary source images, a teacher can focus the guiding questions to encourage students to tailor their analysis to a visual primary source. Questions in Table 3.2 can be used by a teacher who is facilitating an

Table 3.2
Teacher's Guide to Analyzing Primary Source Images in Elementary School

I See . . .	I Think . . .	I Wonder . . .
Use these questions to focus students on identifying details in an image and verbalizing their observations.	*Use these questions to encourage students to react to the image, create hypotheses, and make connections to prior knowledge.*	*Use these questions to prompt students to ask their own unique questions that may bring them back to examine the source more carefully or explore other sources for answers.*
Possible Questions What do you see? What else do you notice? What seems important/ unusual? Are there any words? Is there something that you have never seen before?	What do you think is happening in this image? What do you think this picture shows? What could the people in this picture be doing/ thinking? How might this person be feeling? What did you expect to see that isn't here?	What does this make you wonder about? What would you ask someone in this picture? What would you ask the person who created the image? What questions do you have?
Clarifying Prompts Show me what you see. Point to what you see. Describe what you are seeing.	What do you see that makes you say/think that? Show me what you see that makes you say/think that.	What in the image made you wonder that?

image primary source analysis. Different questions should be used at differing points in the analysis process to encourage students to make observations, reactions, or questions.

Possible questions listed in the guide can help a teacher frame the analysis or transition students to one of the elements of analysis as students examine the image. As students share what they see, think, and wonder, clarifying prompts can be used by the teacher to guide students in verbalizing their thinking. While not all questions in the table would be appropriate for every image, teachers can select ones that work for a particular focus during the analysis strategy.

Puzzle Strategy

Using a puzzle strategy, a teacher breaks up the primary source image into pieces. Typically the parts of the primary source image are enlarged and printed out, or the primary source is printed and cut into pieces. Those pieces are given to individual or pairs of students. It usually only makes sense to break an image into a certain number of pieces. Don't hesitate to give multiple individuals or pairs the same part of the image or combine them into an even larger group. Another option is to create two, three, or four groups within a class where each person in the group has their own piece of the puzzle.

This adaptation to the See, Think, Wonder strategy works well with elementary students when the image has a lot of detail, when enlarging the image can expose that detail, or when the image has distinguishable parts that students would benefit from looking at separately. Maps are often great choices for the Puzzle strategy because of the amount of detail. If analyzing an image with a standard See, Think, Wonder strategy does not work as expected because students overlook areas of the image, try modifying it using the Puzzle strategy the next time the image is used with students.

A student or student group analyzes a piece of the primary source image separately, not knowing what the other pieces of the primary source look like. The See, Think, Wonder strategy is still used here. The strategy is just focused on one aspect of the image. There are two benefits. First, students can take a very close look at one part of the image in their primary source analysis. This often allows them to see more detail than they would have when looking at the entire image. The second is that when students share their findings with others, they are the experts on that part of the image. This gives them a sense of ownership and allows them to offer their unique perspective to the discussion.

After documenting what they see, think, and wonder, the whole class comes together to share their findings and see the entire image. Depending on time and other factors, there are several ways to come together to share learning. One way is for each student or group to share highlights of their analysis, possibly around a prompt or framing of the analysis given by the teacher. After sharing, students can work together to put the pieces together to make the full image. This gives them an opportunity to take a close look at other parts of the image. Another sharing opportunity would be for students or groups to share something from each part of the image in a round-robin format concluding in them constructing the puzzle into the full image. Students may also take a walking tour in the classroom, looking at others' primary source analyses before bringing the entire class together to put together the full image.

A teacher will want to decide how the image is divided for the Puzzle strategy. When using a map, it may make sense to print off sections of the map so that details can be enlarged. Photos or other images with less detail may be printed and cut into smaller pieces. Some images have distinct parts, but those parts may overlap. In that case, it may make sense to divide the image digitally and print each scene of the total image. This may result in some areas being left out that are not important to the analysis. If that is the case, share that information with students as they are putting together the puzzle. They will be able to use the overlapping parts of the image to connect pieces together.

Primary source images can be cut to focus students' attention in using the Puzzle strategy.

Jump In Strategy

In a Jump In strategy, students imagine that they are able to jump into the image. While jumping in, they describe the scene around them, connecting to the moment by placing themselves in it.

This strategy works best with photographs, paintings, or other images that show a clear setting. It can also be helpful when there are people clearly in the image. Photos can make it easier for elementary students to put themselves in a place, imagining what is unknown by connecting to what they do recognize in the photograph. A teacher may have multiple students use the same photograph for a Jump In strategy. He or she may also have a group of related photos taken from the same time or even in the same location that students may jump into.

Students often like to have an individual print of the primary source photograph. It allows them to have a close look as they imagine themselves in the photo. As students share their analysis, it is also good to have the image projected, putting the student near the image so that others can imagine the student in the photo as he or she shares.

To begin the strategy, as part of framing the primary source analysis, a teacher will give students an idea of what they will be sharing when jumping in.

During the Jump In strategy, you are going to imagine yourself actually jumping into the photograph. Look at it carefully. Where will you be standing once you jump in? Who or what will be around you? You will want to imagine that you are really in this place and people are moving, not frozen as in this photo.

The teacher would then ask for a volunteer who would come to the front of the room, standing in front of the projected image. Jump In strategy often works best, especially as students are first experiencing the strategy, if the teacher interviews the student who is imagining himself or herself in the photo. The teacher may start by asking the student to tell the rest of the class a little about the setting. This allows the student to begin sharing observations of the photo. The teacher may follow with asking about sounds, movement, and even smells depending on the image the student is using for the strategy. The purpose is to encourage the student to continue to immerse himself or herself in the moment. The student connects what is seen in the image with his or her own background knowledge to make sense of the event. As students become more comfortable with this strategy, the teacher may ask the student some follow-up questions on the basis of what the student shares. The teacher may also ask a student about imagined conversations had with people in the photo. Even if the student doesn't mention a conversation, the teacher can push the student further into immersing himself or herself in the image.

While this is happening, the teacher may invite other students to react and ask questions to the student who has jumped in. This encourages everyone to be engaged, listening, and observing while allowing students who may not be comfortable performing this type of analysis in front of the class a place to still play a role in the discussion.

The components of the See, Think, Wonder strategy are evident as the student in the Jump In strategy makes observations and reacts to the image by sharing what sounds, sights, or conversations could be happening in the moment the image was captured. For a change of focus more in line of the See, Wonder, Think strategy, ask a student to jump in and begin with other students asking their questions and the student immersing himself or herself in the photo answering them.

For a technologically equipped school, students can actually place themselves in the photo using a green screen along with a device with a camera and software that puts them in the image. Students then can create a product documenting their Jump In experience.

Pose Strategy

In the Pose strategy, students pose themselves like a person in the photo, putting themselves in the shoes of that individual and taking on their role in the context of the primary source image. Students are encouraged to not only put themselves in the posture of the individual but also reflect on what the individual in the photo is thinking, saying, or feeling.

The Pose strategy works well with portraits or images where an individual is able to be fully seen. When selecting a primary source, do not ignore images where the pose seems too typical. Look closely at body language and facial expressions. Any of these may give insights into the person in the image. This can also be done with images of multiple individuals. Costumes, props, or other elements can be available to help the student pose and take on the role of the individual in the image.

Like other image primary source analysis, students can benefit from a printed or digital image as well as a projected image. Using the printed or digital image for the close look helps them examine every aspect of the person in the image. Digitally being able to zoom in may encourage students to study facial expression or something that can otherwise be easily overlooked like the position of a hand or tilt of a head.

Along with framing the purpose of the analysis, the teacher can help students prepare for the Pose strategy by helping them focus their attention on observations of an individual in the image.

> As we work with this primary source image today, I'm going to ask each of you to choose someone in the photo. Select someone who you think may be interesting and that you want to know more about. Look at that person very carefully because you are going to be posing like them, trying, in a way, to become them at this one moment when this photo was taken. Look at how they are standing. Are their feet close together or far apart?
>
> I'm going to ask you to make careful observations. You may even want to stand up as you look at this photo and begin to practice. Where are their hands? Where are they looking? Look closely at their face. I want you to even try to make the exact same facial expression as they are making. I'm going to give you a few minutes to not only look closely, but to practice posing yourself like that person.

Unlike Jump In, the Pose strategy can be done by multiple students at once, especially when they are each taking on the role of one person in a primary source image where several people are shown. Even in an image with one person, multiple students may pose at once.

As students take on the pose, the teacher may ask, as they take on the role of the person in the portrait, what they are thinking or how they are feeling. This encourages the students to connect the observations with their thinking about the individual on the basis of those observations. Of course, students may add details about the setting or about others around them, but unlike Jump In, the idea behind the Pose strategy is not for the student to become immersed in a setting but instead to become immersed in an individual.

Students observing may also comment, making observations about how a student is presenting himself or herself. As they do, they may make comparisons to the primary source image, share their own thoughts on why the person being mirrored has positioned himself or herself in a certain way, or how an individual may be feeling or thinking in that pose.

Analyzing Primary Source Text

Text-based primary sources can be rich resources to bring into an elementary classroom. Learning to read primary source text through a primary source analysis is a different skill than reading the expository text often found in nonfiction books or on websites that students may access for information. The benefit though can be the details found and the puzzles that can be uncovered by analyzing primary source text.

Types of Primary Source Texts

There are almost no limits to the primary source text that students may use. Like images, choices are often dictated though by how topics under study were documented at the time.

In Table 3.3, some of these formats are also listed under primary source images. For some, it may not matter whether a format like a newspaper advertisement is listed as an image or text-based primary source. For other teachers, it may. They may be looking for a specific type of format or possibly are concerned about struggles for their striving readers. Whatever the reason, there is a not-so-simple answer to how these formats should be categorized. It depends. If categorizing a

Table 3.3
Types of Primary Source Text

Letters
Postcards or telegrams
Diary entries
Tabulated data
Written interviews
Posters
Legal or government documents
Patents
Written speeches
Newspaper stories
Newspaper advertisements
Newspaper headlines
Political cartoons

format or a particular primary source is important, consider not only the prominence of the image versus the text but also where students will likely be giving their attention. This will depend on how the teacher frames the primary source analysis, so some initial planning on the potential student learning is helpful.

Considerations When Selecting Primary Source Texts

There are several elements of primary source text that may dissuade a teacher from asking a child to interact with it. Try to look beyond the blockades to the benefits that the text may have. If there are opportunities to make meaning from the text and learn from it, there are ways around the obstacles.

Challenging Vocabulary in Primary Source Texts

It is not unusual to find an engaging piece of primary source text and then notice vocabulary that you know that your elementary students will absolutely not know. There may be words that they likely haven't seen yet, but it is just as likely that the text has words or phrases that are no longer in fashion.

In a search for newspaper articles about early cars, you may find references to an automobile, horseless carriage, motor car, or motocycle. If the teacher believes the majority of students are savvy enough to use context clues to determine the definition, he or she should allow them to do that, being ready to address questions if they arise. If understanding vocabulary is going to be an obstacle, the teacher should support the student by providing vocabulary support for words or phrases.

When a teacher thinks students may need vocabulary support, it should be done from the beginning, not as students ask for it. This avoids unnecessary frustration when working with the primary source and keeps the pacing of the analysis going. Providing vocabulary to previously unknown words and phrases may even begin to engage students in the analysis itself.

An example can be found in the analysis tool created by a fifth-grade teacher for students to analyze a portion of text on a study of colonization shown in Table 3.4. In the passage from the Virginia Company, the words "endeavour" and "burthened" as well as the phrase "goal habitation" were thought to be problematic for the fifth-grade readers. Notice how the vocabulary support is built directly into the transcript of the item and analysis form. Students can seamlessly read, make annotations on the text, react, ask questions, and visit vocabulary support in one document.

The one exception to this suggestion is when the purpose of the primary source analysis is for students to determine the meaning of a new piece of vocabulary. While not entirely text based, students used image-based primary sources to determine the meaning of heliocentric and geocentric. In the lesson, students had multiple images that represented heliocentric models of the solar system. Others had

Table 3.4
Directions to the Colonists from the Virginia Company

"When it shall please God to send you on the coast of Virginia, you shall do your best **endeavour** to find out a safe port in the entrance of some navigable river . . . ." "You must take especial care that you choose a seat for **habitation** that shall not be over **burthened** with woods near your town; for all the men you have . . . ."

GLOSSARY
endeavour—*n.* an attempt to achieve a goal
habitation—*n.* a place in which to live
burthened—(burdened) *v.* heavily loaded

"Neither must you plant in a low or moist place, because it will prove unhealthful. You shall judge of the good air by the people; for some part of that coast where the lands are low, have their people—with swollen bellies and legs; but if the naturals be strong and clean made, it is a true sign of wholesome soil."

MY OBSERVATIONS
Please highlight or underline parts of the text that stand out to you as important or unusual before writing reflections and questions.

MY REFLECTIONS

MY QUESTIONS

---

primary sources that represented geocentric models. The framing of the analysis was to use the text and visual context in the primary sources to determine what those two words meant. In a case like this, the use of context becomes key, and vocabulary support would go against the goals of the lesson. In these cases, primary sources need to be carefully selected to assure that the goal of defining these words can be met with the resources at hand.

These types of vocabulary-focused primary source analyses have two elements in place. First, the purpose of the analysis is to determine the meaning of the vocabulary, and that purpose is evident to the students through the framing of the analysis. Second, there is enough context through one or more primary sources that would lead the teacher to assume that students can define a piece of vocabulary through the analysis of the primary sources.

Handwriting in Primary Source Texts

There are a number of opinions from students, teachers, and parents about the decrease in number of students taught to write in cursive. Interacting with text-based primary sources does not necessitate that students write in cursive, but they

Student uses the context within the primary source to build vocabulary knowledge.

may need to be able to read it. Letters, diary entries, and even government documents may require students to be able to read handwriting to interact with the source.

A teacher does have the option of replacing the letter, diary, or other source with a transcript. If possible, he or she may want to avoid it though. Relying solely on the transcript separates the student from the source possibly making the student less engaged and invested in the analysis. Instead, if a teacher knows that students will be working with a primary source written in cursive, he or she may want to build students' ability to read the letter by giving them a small portion of a handwritten document at a time. This works best with shorter documents or a passage of a longer document. Students may initially take a minute to puzzle through a word but soon build up to taking the same amount of time with an entire sentence.

When time comes for the analysis, students can be paired or grouped so that they can support each other in reading the document. The teacher can be available to be a resource in the reading. Students may want to create their own transcript or transcribe words they find particularly difficult to read. This time to interact with the source will also give them a chance to tune into language used, new vocabulary, and the overall message of the text.

These types of documents will likely be used by upper-elementary students. Teachers will want to consider the length of the document. If it is critical to use a longer document where the cursive handwriting will be a struggle, a transcript used alongside the source may be the wisest choice.

The Long S in Primary Source Texts

Anyone who has taught with primary source text from the 18th century has seen the long S that is often interpreted as an F by students when they first read these documents. This misreading can cause confusion or frustration in upper-elementary students who may see these texts in a U.S. history unit. This may lead a teacher to not use the items at all or to transcribe them for students.

While transcription is an option, a teacher should be encouraged to share the original piece alongside the recreated one. Another option is for the students to practice reading similar text with the long S to become more accustomed to the letter formation. Interacting with short passages from a primer from the time period can give students exposure to the long S (see Figure 3.5). Students could interact with the primer multiple times over the course of a week or more, reading or transcribing with a partner. The more exposure they have, the greater likelihood that, just like reading handwriting, they will become more fluent in reading these texts allowing them to focus on making connections with the primary source and not struggling with reading it.

Figure 3.5
18th-Century Primer.

Long Passages of Primary Source Text

There may be a text-based primary source that a teacher wants students to read and analyze, but he or she feels the text is too long. Letters, newspaper articles, diary entries, and transcripts of interviews can be some of the formats that a teacher may struggle with because of the length. The labor may be with the students' ability to comprehend the complexities in a longer piece of text. Another concern could be the time that is taken for students to read and analyze a lengthy piece of text, especially on a topic that is new to them. A growing list of unknown vocabulary or terminology could also cause a teacher to pause.

A question that teachers have asked is whether selecting just a piece of the text is restricting a student from understanding the primary source itself. It would be unlikely that a teacher would show a fraction of a photograph or corner of a map without at some point revealing the full image. This same solution may not be viable for elementary students when working with primary source text. It is not something that should be sent home as homework. Even if time is allowed, analyzing a long piece of text over days would likely be exhausting to students, engagement would soon wane, and the analysis would become more of a chore than a motivation to learn from a compelling source. What can a teacher do?

An option is to use a portion of the primary source text. When considering this option, a teacher should think about whether a portion of the text truly represents the learning that he or she wants for the students. The teacher should also think about whether the portion of the primary source text represents the text as a whole and does not give a misrepresentation of the overall message the author of the piece is trying to convey. If both of these are met, the teacher may find natural breaking points and share a portion of the text with the students.

The teacher should also keep in mind that there needs to be enough of a passage for students to analyze. Taking one sentence or a short quotable piece does not usually give students enough to make meaning from because they are not able to rely on context to fully understand the passage. If students only have time to analyze a sentence or short passage, he or she can supply the text in its entirety or a large amount of it for students to access while analyzing the smaller part of the primary source text.

The one exception to the suggestions on avoiding the use of short passages may be when using newspaper headlines. These short pieces of text are meant to convey large amounts of information in a few words. Using a close reading strategy with headlines can convey information about an event as well as the perspective of the newspaper where it appears. Analyzing multiple headlines from several newspapers or headlines from one newspaper over time as an event unfolds can provide students a general understanding of that event that then can be broadened with other primary sources or secondary sources.

Images in Primary Source Text

There are a number of primary sources where the text is the prevalent way that information is shared but an image appears alongside it. Letters with sketches, advertisements, and cartoons are some examples where this can happen. A teacher may ask students to do two primary source analyses or mesh both into one. These two choices can be exhausting or confusing for the students.

Instead, the teacher should determine what is the main focus of the analysis. Students should analyze that element of the primary source using whatever analysis strategy the teacher or students choose. If focusing on text, they may use the See, Think, Wonder strategy. As students finish their initial analysis, the teacher can ask students to revisit the source and focus on the other element.

> You just spent your time analyzing the text of this newspaper advertisement, but there was more to this particular advertisement than just the text. There was also an image. Even though the text gives most of the information, there was a reason that the person who created this advertisement included an image.
>
> Let's do a shorter analysis looking at how the image may change our understanding of the text or make us feel even more certain about the message of this advertisement.
>
> First, I'd like to you make observations about the image. You have done this with other images, so this should be a familiar step. After you do that, revisit your thinking statements and questions in the text analysis. Do the observations of the image change anything about how you think about the advertisement or questions you have of it? No need to erase anything if you have changed your thinking. Just add your new thinking and questions to what you already have.

Revisiting after a second round of observations can allow students to organize their thinking. After having this experience several times, the teacher may want to combine the analysis of the two elements but offer two columns for observations for students to document text and image observations separately.

Student Interactions with Primary Source Texts

Determining How Students Will Interact with the Source

Like images, students can work with primary source text in print, digital, or projected forms. Also like images, there are benefits and drawbacks to each that can be taken into consideration. Regardless of the strategy, a teacher may tailor the framing and questions specifically for primary source text. The can help direct students in observations, interpretations, and questions that stem from the text.

Table 3.5
Teacher's Guide to Analyzing Primary Source Text in Elementary School

I See . . .	I Think . . .	I Wonder . . .
Use these questions to focus students on identifying details in an image and verbalizing their observations.	*Use these questions to encourage students to react to the image, create hypotheses, and make connections to prior knowledge.*	*Use these questions to prompt students to ask their own unique questions that may bring them back to examine the source more carefully or explore other sources for answers.*
Possible Questions What words do you notice first? What is being described? Are there names, places, or people that are familiar? What words or phrases seem important/unusual/unexpected? What words or phrases are strange or unfamiliar? How is the text arranged on the page? What is on the page besides writing?	Why do you think this was written? Who do you think wrote this? Who do you think this was written for? What do you think was happening at the time this was written? What do you think the point of view was of the person who wrote this?	What does this make you wonder about? What would you ask the person who wrote this? What questions do you have?
Clarifying Prompts Read me the text you're talking about. Point to the text. What do you think that word/ phrase means?	What are you reading that makes you say/think that? Read me the text that makes you say/think that.	What in the text made you wonder that?

The Teacher's Guide to Analyzing Primary Source Text in Elementary School (Table 3.5) may help a teacher focus his or her questioning to students when working with primary source text. The questions are meant to bring out observations, reactions, and questions related to the text and prompts that can be used to ask students to clarify their thinking that they share. These also can be modified to fit the needs of the teacher and student during the analysis.

Printed copies of text-based primary sources can have benefits for student analysis. As students make individual observations, they can underline or box around a piece of text instead of rewriting it. Related questions or thinking about the passage can typically be written in the margins. If students are reading transcripts alongside a handwritten primary source, being able to look closely at the original print may help them focus on the letters and words as they are reading the piece.

There are also advantages to elementary students reading text-based primary sources in a digital format. Digital viewing allows upper-elementary students to scroll through longer passages. A teacher may also be able to isolate a passage or a source from other material if he or she does not want the students to see other parts of the primary source immediately. If using a transcript, students may be able to view it together in a shared document where they can add notes to highlighted portions of the text, allowing everyone to see their thinking.

Projected primary source text can be viewed by the entire class. This gives students more chance for collaborative analysis as a group and is a way to share out thinking after working with a print or digital document they were viewing in isolation or with a small group. Ultimately, there may be great reason for students to have a close look and group look at a primary source text if resources allow.

Transcripts of Primary Source Text

Transcripts have already been mentioned earlier in this chapter. A teacher may choose to use them when students are analyzing a text-based primary source that is handwritten. Some primary sources come with transcripts, but a teacher may choose to create a transcript for a source that does not. When creating the transcript, the teacher will want to think about how the transcript allows young students to move between the original source and the transcript.

The most simple transcript is a block of text. For shorter text-based primary source documents, this may be a simple approach that is quick for a teacher to create. To help student move between the two documents, the teacher may put them on the same printed page. Another way to help students move between transcript and original primary source is to create line breaks in the transcript at the same place as the original document. Numbering those lines on the transcript and even over the print of the original primary source encourages students to move between original source and transcript.

Multipage letters may have the transcript coded or marked by page. This could allow students to read the original document and, if there is a struggle with a word or phrase, to easily transition to the transcript.

Jigsaw Strategy

An option when working with longer passages of primary source text may be to jigsaw the primary source. A teacher may choose this approach if students are already experienced in a strategy to analyze primary source text, and the longer primary source text naturally breaks into sections that match up with a number of smaller groups that can be made in class.

Unlike a traditional jigsaw where one student works with one piece of information within the larger group, when analyzing a primary source text, it is often

Transcripts of a primary source can be viewed with the original document.

helpful to have two students working together during the analysis. An example would be a classroom where there are three jigsaw groups where each group is made up of four pairs. After analyzing their section of the primary source text, each pair meets in expert groups to solidify their understanding of their portion of the text. Pairs then return to their original jigsaw group. Each pair shares their analysis of their part of the text. A protocol could allow for a brief question and answer after each sharing. This gives pairs within each jigsaw group an opportunity to clarify understanding and make connections to their own text. The teacher may want to provide support with vocabulary or terminology as well.

Writing a Headline to Summarize

One suggestion from Harvard's Project Zero that works well with elementary students is to summarize a text-based primary source with a headline. It is, of course, helpful for students to understand what a headline is. Viewing them in magazines, online stories, or even newspapers from today can give students an idea of the brevity that is used and the idea that a headline can highlight an aspect of the text while summarizing a larger portion. Students can work in small groups to create the headline, and headlines from multiple groups can be shared, explained, and then displayed along with the text. The headline may help the teacher as a formative assessment to understand how students' thinking is related to the primary source text.

Analyzing Primary Source Sounds and Moving Pictures

Primary source sounds and moving pictures may not be the first format of primary source that a teacher decides to use. There are some inherent challenges to overcome, so for it to be worthwhile to teachers, there should also be inherent benefits for student learning in an elementary setting.

Types of Primary Source Sounds and Moving Pictures

One could easily say that this format of primary source would include television, film, and audio recordings. The list in Table 3.6 attempts to show the wide variety within that shorter list that elementary teachers may think about using with their students.

You may notice that some of these primary sources may exist as both audio and video formats depending on how the individual or event was documented. It is also interesting that many may also exist in a text or image format. A television commercial may also appear as a print advertisement for the same product using the same slogan. Recorded interviews may also exist as text-based transcripts. Speeches may exist as an audio recording and also be found in print in a newspaper. Even recorded music may have accompanying sheet music.

One type of primary source that many may not be familiar with is actuality film. It was a popular type of film in the late 19th and early 20th century as films were

Table 3.6
Types of Primary Source Sounds and Moving Pictures

Television programs
Television commercials
Home movies
Actuality films
Newsreel films
Video or audio oral histories
Video or audio news reports
Video or audio interviews
Video or audio speeches
Recorded music
Comedic recordings

---

new. Companies such as Edison Studios would capture minutes or sometimes even seconds worth of film showing moments of actual life. Unlike a documentary, these were much shorter and did not have an overall message. These films, many showing bustling cities or man-made marvels, were shown across the country and were a popular introduction to the film experience for many. They fell out of favor after a fairly short period of time as films later became ways to tell stories. The benefit to these actuality films is that they give us a window into lives during that moment in history. Many actuality films have been digitized and are available through the Library of Congress.

Considerations When Selecting Primary Source Sounds and Moving Pictures

It seems that what may inhibit a teacher from using audiovisual primary sources are what many educators are concerned about in general when planning learning, technology and time. There is no paper version of a recorded sound clip or video although the print alternatives mentioned earlier may be helpful when barriers stop a teacher from using these formats in the classroom. While time and technology may slow a teacher from selecting an audiovisual primary source, it should not stop him or her. The following are considerations for teachers to take into account, many of which may tip the scales toward bringing recorded audio and video into the classroom.

Time Available to Interact with the Source

Time can be a major factor that elementary teachers pose when concerned about analyzing a primary source with students. Time should be a consideration when students may analyze an audiovisual primary source.

Unlike a photo analysis where a teacher can easily shorten the time students will have to view the image, an audiovisual primary source has a set time that it needs to play. Beyond that, students will need time to view or listen to the source multiple times to make their observations, react to the source, and generate questions. Depending on the length of time of the piece, the complexity, and how carefully students are analyzing it, students can listen to or view a piece several times. Because of this, a teacher may want to seek out shorter audiovisual clips for students to analyze, allowing time for the primary source to be heard or viewed multiple times within the class time allowed.

Supporting Sound of the Primary Source

Sound can be a factor when listening to an audiovisual primary source. We have all heard, or tried to hear, those family videos or student-created projects that had poor sound quality. Equipment and sound quality can be a factor with audio-visual primary sources. Digitized audio records can contain pops, hisses, and scratches that make the audio difficult to hear. Original audio recordings may have been digitized in a way to cause them to play more softly than originally intended. Some classroom sound systems are limited, and it may be challenging to hear over the murmur of students analyzing the source.

When selecting a primary source with recorded audio, the teacher will want to take these limitations into account while also thinking about how to overcome them if there is a benefit to bringing the primary source into the classroom. Equipment needs will be explored later, but a teacher may also think about creating a transcript to accompany audiovisual primary sources with spoken words. This will allow students to read along with the audio, still hearing the inflections that may impact how the piece is interpreted without being distracted by straining to hear the piece itself.

Movement within the Primary Source

One of the advantages to using a film is the movement. Why look at photos of early automobiles if you can see a film of them zipping through the streets of a busy city? Students can look at photos of groups of immigrants coming to the United States at the turn of the 19th century, but being able to watch them as they carry their belongings from the ship also has an impact. Written accounts of the civil rights movement are powerful, but seeing those individuals march allows us not only to put ourselves in their shoes but to walk in them just for a moment.

If a teacher wants to explore interactions between people or objects and their environment, he or she should consider looking for film or video of the event. Like other formats, a teacher can predict what students will notice when looking at the movement within primary source film and video and how they will interpret that movement on the screen. If those noticings and interpretations can impact the learning from the analysis in a way that an image or text will not, consider it for the classroom.

Emotion Shown through the Primary Source

Powerful emotions can be seen in a photograph. The same can be said around word choice in a letter. Hearing someone speak, seeing their expressions, and hearing and seeing others react to that person can provide many layers of emotion in a primary source. These can come across in visual elements like film and video as well as audio recordings on records or other medium.

A teacher may be hesitant to focus on feelings and emotions that are implied through voice and body language. It is important for students to describe what they see or hear that makes them think an emotion is being shown by someone in an audiovisual primary source. Students may not all agree someone is happy, but they can agree that they saw a smile or heard a laugh.

In addition, students can be encouraged to notice those sounds and actions that are reactions and show emotions. Laughs, groans, gasps, wide eyes, tears, and other elements are best seen and heard in an audiovisual primary source. If students focus on an individual, as they are likely to do, a teacher can suggest they also see how others are reacting to and around that individual.

The Teacher's Guide to Analyzing Primary Source Audiovisuals in Elementary School (Table 3.7) focuses observation questions on the emotion and movement

Table 3.7
Teacher's Guide to Analyzing Primary Source Audiovisuals in Elementary School

I See ...	I Think ...	I Wonder ...
Use these questions to focus students on identifying details in an image and verbalizing their observations.	*Use these questions to encourage students to react to the image, create hypotheses, and make connections to prior knowledge.*	*Use these questions to prompt students to ask their own unique questions that may bring them back to examine the source more carefully or explore other sources for answers.*
Possible Questions		
What do you see/hear?	What do you think is	What does this make you
What is being said?	happening in this film/	wonder about?
What emotions can we	recording?	What would you ask
hear in the voice?	Why do you think this was	someone in this film/
What movement do you	created?	recording?
see on the screen?	What do you think may be	What would you ask the
What is happening in the	important about the	person who created the film/
background that might	background?	recording?
be important?	What do you think this film/	What questions do you
What other details can	audio shows?	have?
you see/hear?	What could the people in	
Are there any words/text	this film/audio be doing/	
in the film?	thinking?	
	How might this person be	
	feeling?	
	What did you expect to see/	
	hear that you didn't?	
Clarifying Prompts		
When did you see/hear that	What do you see/hear that	What in the film/recording
in the source?	makes you say/think that?	made you wonder that?
	Show me what you see/hear	
	that makes you say/think that.	

that can be seen and heard in audiovisual primary sources. These observations can be built upon in reactions and questions as students continue through the analysis process.

Equipment Needed to Interact with Audiovisual Primary Sources

Equipment is an additional factor that teachers must consider when bringing in audiovisual primary sources. While there are a growing number of schools and districts that have one-to-one environments in elementary schools, it is definitely not the norm. It is more likely that students have their own headphones to listen to recorded sound, film, or video, but the teacher should also think about speakers that can be used if students listen to a source as a class.

Many teachers work around their technology limitations. The use of audiovisual primary sources in the elementary classroom is no exception. The next section makes suggestions for students interacting with primary source sounds and moving pictures. The suggestions may need to be altered to meet a classroom's technology footprint. As those alterations are made, a teacher can keep in mind elements of interaction, close looking and listening, and collaboration that show themselves through all types of primary source analysis.

Student Interactions with Primary Source Sounds and Moving Pictures

Student interaction with primary source sounds and moving pictures in an elementary school may be unique compared to other formats of primary sources as well as other audio and video in the classroom. Thinking about how students interact with and react to an audiovisual source will help guide how students learn from this format of primary source.

Active versus Passive Use

One noticeable difference in how students are asked to interact with an audiovisual primary source compared to how they typically interact with audio and video is that they are asked to be active participants in the process. Think about students' typical use of these formats throughout the day out of school. They are consuming the product, often for entertainment. While they may be asked to summarize or react to a video or audio recording in class, audiovisual primary source analysis asks them to take those skills and turn them up, often watching and rewatching to make their observations, focusing in on small moments, movements, words, and sounds.

That level of active analysis may be new to many students and will take practice. Choosing short audiovisual primary sources to analyze will make that practice meaningful and manageable. Giving students control of the primary source will allow them to determine where they focus their attention. Having varied options for documenting the analysis will enable students to vocalize their analysis, tying it to the visual or heard moment in the audiovisual source.

Students may be challenged to focus throughout even a short audiovisual primary source. Scaffolding the analysis by giving students a written transcript of the audio or a written overview of the scenes in the video can help students focus on the moment while also knowing where they are within the larger context of the audio or film. These types of supports also give students something to document their analysis directly on while watching or listening to the source.

Student Control of Access to the Primary Source

It is important, especially with longer audiovisual primary sources, to give a student control of the primary source itself. Just as a student can have a copy of an image or newspaper article to look at closely and focus on a certain point, a student also benefits from his or her own device to view or listen to an audiovisual primary source. Having his or her own desktop, laptop, or tablet gives the student the ability to play, stop, or rewind. It allows watching or listening to a small moment multiple times or playing the source over from the beginning. A student can focus the analysis on a moment in a film or a sentence in a speech. Having his or her own devices empowers the student to do this when analyzing an audiovisual source.

Of course, not all students have access to a one-to-one environment, even for a short period of time. When that is the case, working in pairs or very small groups can be an alternative. This option also works well when students could benefit from a thinking partner during an audiovisual primary source analysis.

There may be times when a whole-class analysis is the preferred option to analyze an audiovisual primary source. This may be due to the equipment available, time available for the analysis, or the desire of the teacher to model through a whole-class analysis. If this is the case, consider replaying the audio or video multiple times, providing transcripts if necessary, or taking requests to play certain moments from the source for students that they want to revisit. All of these options give students opportunities to look more carefully at an audiovisual primary source.

Documenting Primary Source Audio Analysis

Analysis methods do not necessarily change as elementary students analyze recorded audio, but how they document their analysis can be specialized. Factors such as the age of students, their familiarity with primary source analysis, and available technology can influence how the teacher decided how the students will document their analysis.

If possible, a student should be able to rewind, stop, and replay an audiovisual primary source.

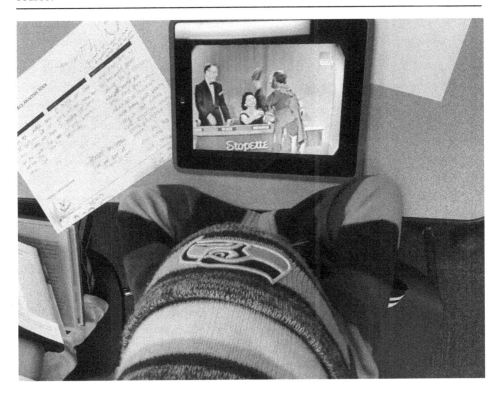

Many students will likely document their analysis on paper. If the audio source is text-heavy, a transcript provided by the teacher can allow students to quickly identify text that they want to highlight as part of their analysis. Students can annotate around the transcript to show other sounds, reactions to the audio, or questions. Writing this in connection with the text in the transcript allows students a way to connect a thought or question to a direct moment in the audio. A teacher may even include time stamps in the transcript to return to a specific moment quickly.

Another way to document on paper is to have students write down text or other audio they hear that they feel is important to the analysis. This encourages students to focus on small moments that impact them as they listen, documenting what is important to them through the analysis. This option works well when students have control to replay portions of the audio on their own device.

If students have software available to record their voice and manipulate the primary source audio, they can also document their analysis in an audio recording. The final product may begin with the source and then have portions of student-recorded audio interjected in as commentary as they share observations, reactions, or questions. This obviously requires a certain technological skill and is more likely to be an option for upper-elementary students. This can also be the most time-intensive option for primary source audio analysis.

Documenting Primary Source Video and Film Analysis

Like audio, primary source video and film analysis follows the same strategies, but documenting the analysis encourages creative options as students try to document and comment on moments across the moving image. It is possible, especially for the youngest students, to analyze a film together verbally—pausing at moments where students want to point out observations, make comments, or ask questions. As students become more sophisticated in their ability to record their analysis, there are other options.

If the film or video is simply a person talking and the teacher believes there is nothing significant in the visual elements, he or she should use the aforementioned suggestions for documenting the analysis of primary source audio.

There are other options if visual elements are important to the analysis. When recording on paper, a teacher can give students still images from the video or film as a place to document their analysis. The benefit is that the students have a simple visual to connect their writing to. The drawback is that the moments are captured by the teacher. There may be other moments in the video or film that better show what students want to focus on in their analysis. Older students who have individual devices can capture those moments in screenshots and anchor their written analysis around those moments.

Another option for written documentation is for students to sketch and write about moments in the film or video they want to document. This low-tech option gives the teacher insights into what few moments the students determine are key as they make meaning of the audiovisual primary source. Students being able to rewatch or pause the source is key to students having time to document their analysis using this method.

Finally, for upper-elementary students who have access to video-editing software, students can document their video or film analysis by importing it into the editing software and documenting their analysis through the film. This may be done by placing text over the video in the software. Students may also record audio over the digital file documenting their observations, reactions, and questions. Recording audio works especially well in silent films.

While analysis does not change greatly, how students interact with the source and document their analysis can change depending on the format of primary source that students use. Teachers may begin sharing one format of primary source with students and then expand into different formats as students become comfortable and as opportunities arise.

Chapter 4

Connecting Primary Sources to Content Curriculum

In my library I have opportunities to connect to student learning through many subject areas. As I began to bring primary sources into my instruction, social studies became a natural fit. Many of my students' experiences connected with their classroom social studies curriculum, and several teachers began working with primary sources in their classrooms in the same subject.

As I continued to explore new sources, talk with elementary teachers about curriculum, and read what others were doing with primary sources in high school and middle school classes outside of social studies, my ideas expanded. I began to see the benefits of learning with primary sources in language arts, science, and math. Opportunities for cross-subject learning opened. Students began encountering primary sources in almost every subject area.

Connections happened in many ways. I looked for moments when using primary sources enhanced the learning experience. When those opportunities came, the hunt was on for primary sources and strategies that would connect to the instruction that was already happening. Sometimes a teacher approached me who had a lesson or part of a unit that was not as successful as he or she hoped and thought primary sources might play a role in improving instruction. Other times I came across sources that I knew would be a perfect fit for a topic of study, and I would approach a teacher to collaborate on how it could be brought in.

I continue to look for opportunities to bring primary sources into different subject areas. Not only does it enhance student learning but it also gives a richer experience as primary sources are used with other resources in the classroom.

A word of warning prior to reading this chapter. As students are encouraged to ask their own questions and make their own observations and meaning from a primary source or set of sources, they may become engaged in a specific area of the general topic of study that deviates from where the teacher thought the primary source analysis would lead them.

My hope is that a teacher can be open to slight variations from the topic originally intended. The teacher can consider whether the engagement justifies explored learning in an area related to what was planned. That may mean that the teacher has to leave behind planned activities to help the student find new resources to continue the learning. Often though, these new directions can be invigorating to the teacher as well as a memorable learning experience for students with primary sources. Expect the unexpected!

Viewing Primary Sources through a Subject Area Lens

The final consideration as a teacher prepares a primary-source-analysis activity for students is to connect to other learning (Figure 4.1). This, in many ways, is the most important consideration. Connecting primary source analysis to learning provides purpose for the learning beyond the analysis itself. Primary source analysis should not exist in a silo. Connecting to student learning may also cause a teacher to consider primary source analysis. A teacher may have a lesson that isn't meeting the students' needs. Another may struggle to find resources to teach a piece of the curriculum the way he or she wants. Other times, there is a connection to a past event, and the teacher wonders if there are primary sources that may be related.

Certain primary sources lend themselves to certain subject areas, but how a teacher looks at a primary source may lead him or her to consider using it with students in a subject not initially considered. Trey Smith, a former Science Teacher in Residence for the Library of Congress, speaks about teachers viewing primary sources through subject area lenses. He encourages teachers to be even more specific. Within science, how would a biologist look at a specific primary source?

Figure 4.1
Considerations Graphic.

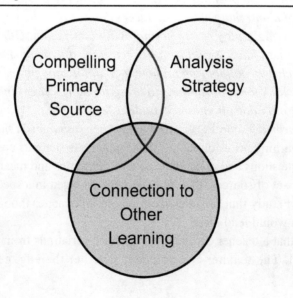

A chemist? A physicist? Looking through that disciplinary lens, what would that type of scientist notice? How would they make meaning from the source? What questions would they ask?

The same logic can be brought to other subject areas. How would an elementary teacher look at a source through the lens of a social studies teacher? Looking at specific areas, what about a historian, economist, or geographer? What sources would be more appealing because they reveal interesting observations or questions when looking through those very specific lenses?

In language arts, a teacher may view sources through the lens of a reader of literature, seeing what primary sources help him or her make sense of the story being read. He or she can take on the role of the author and look at sources through that lens, considering the path the author of a piece may have taken when seeing primary sources to become informed enough to write the piece. In certain cases, the teacher may look through the lens of an illustrator to reveal inspiration and historical accuracy through the use of primary sources. These insights, when that lens is transferred from teacher to student, can help them understand the written word better as well as the work of the author and illustrator.

Though a bit more challenging, primary sources can also be looked at by a teacher through a math lens. At the elementary level, as the teacher looks through the lens, he or she may be considering authentic math situations that can be seen in the primary sources and connecting them with skills his or her students learn throughout the year.

This may not be done through a single source. When we look at a topic under study, there are likely many sources that are available in a variety of different formats. Some of these primary sources may lend themselves to one subject area more than another, while another group of sources may be easily used across subject areas depending on the lens the teacher views them through.

Elementary teachers who teach multiple subject areas have a unique opportunity to bring these sources to their students not just in social studies but in multiple subject areas throughout the school day. This can give students the chance to approach a source through the different lenses that the teacher saw them through, opening the door for new learning from one or a group of primary sources.

A clarifying note: Trey Smith's use of the word "lens" may be confused with the same word in the Close Reading strategy. The action a teacher takes of looking at a primary source through a subject area or discipline lens is not a strategy or part of an analysis strategy. Instead, it is a way to view primary sources as they are being selected for student use. The perspective gained not only leads to a compelling primary source being used in the classroom but it also gives the teacher insight into how he or she hopes students will interact with the primary source. This insight helps the teacher frame the analysis regardless of what analysis strategy is used.

The remainder of this chapter will revolve around a group of primary sources and propose ways they could be used in connection with different subject areas. These connections may span multiple grade levels. The goal is not meant to be a holistic learning experience that one grade level would use across multiple subject areas or one librarian would use across multiple grade levels. Instead, it is meant to illustrate how a teacher may look through specific lenses to determine why and how these primary sources could be used in a specific subject area.

The sources revolve around one historical event: the trip of Nell Richardson and Alice Burke across America by car in 1916. The two suffragists, in an attempt to raise awareness for the women's suffrage movement and upcoming demonstrations at the Democratic and Republican National Conventions, drove from New York to California and back. They stopped in cities along the way and were reported on in newspapers across the United States.

Primary Sources and Social Studies

What may cause a teacher to explore these sources in an elementary social studies lesson? While elementary students do not often study early 20th century history, this event may be studied under civics curriculum in a social studies curriculum. Specifically, a teacher may look at curriculum standards around the role of citizens in the United States and may find himself or herself asking the following questions:

- What are the important responsibilities of Americans?
- What are the important rights of Americans?
- How do citizens participate in their government?
- How do Americans select leaders?

Given these questions, the teacher has a lens that he or she can look through when viewing different primary sources. Reading newspaper stories about the event from the day, the teacher may ask himself or herself the following questions:

- How does this primary source show the two women playing a civic role as citizens?
- How does the source illustrate the rights being sought after through the suffrage movement?
- Is it clear how the women are participating in government through this news story?
- Are parts of government and the roles they play brought forward in this story?

These questions may lead the teacher to a source that highlights these elements. Newspaper articles from the time may highlight this specific event in the larger

Figure 4.2
May 28, 1916, *Arizona Republic*.

Miss Nell Richardson Explains Why National Suffrage Union Can Be for Amendment and Oppose Congressional Union

Back of the Susan B. Anthony amendment is the National Suffrage Association and if that organization shows the grit and determination to pass the national suffrage amendment that its representatives, Mrs. Alice S. Burke and Miss Nell Richardson have demonstrated in securing the endorsement of the suffrage states the measure should carry.

context of voting rights. Articles that highlight the purpose of the trip, to garner support for upcoming demonstrations and to raise awareness, can encourage questions about whether Nell Richardson and Alice Burke were ultimately successful. These questions can also lead to broader questions about Americans historically demonstrating for their right to vote.

One primary source that may encourage a civics focus is a May 28, 1916, article from the *Arizona Republic* (Figure 4.2). The article clearly shares the overall plan of the organization that Nell Richardson and Alice Burke are representing on their journey. It also mentions conflicting organizations working toward women's suffrage and highlights the purpose behind the two suffragists' trip across the United States. The language and message are accessible to most upper-elementary students, especially when working collaboratively.

There may be other lenses to look through as primary sources are selected. Viewing the articles through the lens of a historian may shift his or her view. The teacher can focus on historical perspectives of individuals and institutions within the broader context of American citizens and the right to vote. Broader questions that guide instruction may include the following:

- How do institutions impact individuals? How do individuals impact institutions?
- What cultural positions do institutions have? How are those identified?
- How are institutions created to respond to individuals' needs or changed to respond to individuals' needs?

Viewing the newspaper reporting on the event as an institution, the teacher may explore the news articles through a lens that focuses on the following questions:

- How are this event and the participants in it represented through newspapers, and how do we view that historically?
- Whose voice is not heard in the reporting of this event through the sources?
- What cultural elements are shown, and how do they differ from today?
- What role did this event play in the larger context of women's suffrage in the United States?

The use of language and how the women and their trip were described can be investigated by using a Close Reading strategy explored in Chapter 2. Word choice may reveal whether the author of the story appeared to be supportive of women's suffrage and the goals of this particular event. Students may also wonder if this is the stance of the newspaper.

The idea of voice comes across strong in an April 6, 1916, article from the *Evening Public Ledger* in Philadelphia (Figure 4.3). In this particular article, the women are described as *beauties*, *the prettiest suffragists*, and *passengers* even though they are the only two in the vehicle. A teacher may consider this an interesting article for analysis because there is strong language to be found; patterns in that language could be identified by students; and it will likely be engaging for students to find that pattern, react to it, and discuss how the people and event are being representing by the newspaper.

Finally, since the event involves a trip across the United States, there may be geographic questions that can be asked about the sources. Like historically based questions, they can connect to overarching understandings in the social studies geography curriculum. A teacher may consider the following larger questions:

- How does geography impact people's decisions?
- How do people impact or change geography to make their lives easier?
- How are cultures different in varied geographic regions? How does geography help shape culture?

Questions the teacher may ask specific to the primary source analysis could include the following:

- Where did these women travel as they crossed the country, and do we have ideas of why they may have traveled there?
- What cities reported the travels of the women? Was there a difference in how the event was reported across the country?
- How did the geography of their trip impact timing and travel?

Figure 4.3
April 6, 1916, Philadelphia *Evening Public Ledger.*

SUFFRAGISTS' "GOLDEN FLYER" BEGINS ITS TRIP

New York Beauties Passengers in Auto—Will Stop Here

NEW YORK, April 6.—A low, racing automobile, painted yellow, draped with orange-colored ribbons and occupied by two of the prettiest suffragists that ever demanded the ballot, left New York today for San Francisco to carry arguments for suffrage all the way across the continent. Mrs. Alice Burke, of New York, will drive the car. Her companion is Miss Nell Richardson, of Winchaster, Va.

The "golden flyer," as the car was christened by Mrs. Carrie Chapman Catt, president of the National Woman's Suffrage Association, was escorted part of the way by a procession of automobiles bearing suffragists, who cheered, waved banners and threw kisses at the departing campaigners.

Mrs. Burke and her companion, on the way to and from San Francisco, expect to make speeches or otherwise work for suffrage in the following cities: Philadelphia, Baltimore, Chicago, New Orleans, San Francisco, Los Angeles, Seattle, Detroit and many others.

One way for students to extend their analysis is to map the trip of the two women on the basis of the news stories. Looking from the trip to those institutions reporting it, students plotting points of where stories were reported will give one view of where the story was reported as well as who was likely reading about the trip. Using the Close Reading analysis as a starting-off point, students can plot on a map the different perceived opinions of articles as for or against Nell Richardson and Alice Burke's trip. Students can look for geographic patterns in the opinions. It is important to point out that the newspapers available through Chronicling America are not exhaustive but can still allow students to explore geographic patterns on the basis of reporting.

One newspaper article a teacher may choose that provides a jumping-off point is from the May 27, 1916, *Evening Herald* from Klamath Falls, Oregon (Figure 4.4). It gives an overview of cities where the suffragists will travel. Using an online

Figure 4.4
May 27, 1916, Klamath Falls *Evening Herald*.

Off to Get Votes for Women

Miss Nell Richardson   **Mrs. Alice Snitzer Burke**

Mrs. Alice Snitzer Burke and Miss Nell Richardson, two well known suffragettes, are booked for a journey of 10,000 miles in a little yellow car to stir up "Votes for Women." Leaving New York, they will head for New Orleans, and go on through the Southwest to Los Angeles and up the Pacific coast to San Francisco and Seattle. They start back by way of Minneapolis, Chicago and Detroit.

They will try to arouse the suffragettes over the country to the importance of the "Walkless Parade," which is to take place in St. Louis when the democratic national convention meets.

The automobile itself is calculated to create a favorable impression wherever it goes. It is a gorgeous yellow, with white slip covers, doors of "campaign blue," boasts pocket vases of flowers, yellow flag sticks and "Votes for Women" banners and a chesty American eagle on the radiator. The trunks contain an assortment of tools, suffrage literature, reception gowns and food tablets.

mapping site, students can easily estimate the miles traveled against the 10,000 suggested in the article. Further investigation with primary source news articles can provide additional details of the travel that can refine the students' estimates.

While looking through different discipline lenses within social studies, these primary sources will tie back to the civics standards within this teacher's grade-level social studies curriculum. Why should he or she then bring in the lenses of history and geography? First, it is likely that there are grade-level social studies standards under these two disciplines. Looking through these lenses to connect to overarching understandings about history and geography allows a teacher to identify primary sources that are rich in their ability to connect to student curriculum. These lenses also give the teacher different ideas of how to frame the primary source analysis that students will perform on these sources and how that analysis will connect to other learning.

A teacher viewing through a civics, historical, or geographic lens will be a first step in bringing primary sources into the elementary social studies classroom. After viewing sources through the lens of different disciplines and determining the framing of the analysis, a teacher would likely choose where in the larger unit or lesson the primary source analysis would take place. These considerations will be explored in Chapter 5. He or she will also choose a primary-source-analysis strategy or variation of a strategy written about in Chapter 2. The teacher will have then completed the three key steps of selecting a source, strategy, and connecting primary source analysis to other learning.

Primary Sources and Language Arts

Bringing primary sources into language arts may not seem like a natural choice, but when looking through lenses, great connections can be made. A teacher may consider viewing primary sources through the lens of a reader, writer, or illustrator. Viewing these lenses asks the teacher to consider pairing a book or other literature with the primary sources. Books that have a historical context, either nonfiction or historical fiction, are likely choices. These secondary source pieces of literature could even spur the teacher to seek out related primary sources.

For our example, our group of primary sources was inspired by a picture book *Around America to Win the Vote* by Mara Rockliff. The book tells the story of Alice Burke and Nell Richardson and their journey. Picture books can make good pairings with primary sources at elementary grade levels. The books are often short, typically 32 pages, while still focusing on a historical event or individual.

Looking through the lens of a reader, a teacher may consider the following elements of reading:

- Comprehension
- Setting
- Character
- Engagement

As the teacher views the primary sources through the lens of the reader, he or she can consider when the primary source will be used with respect to the secondary source picture book to positively impact students' engagement with the book. The two typical options are before or after, either introducing the elements through primary sources prior to reading the book or exploring them in more depth and reconnecting with the information from the picture book by using primary sources after. Regardless of where they are used, the teacher may consider certain questions when viewing primary sources in connection with the picture book.

- Does the primary source help illustrate aspects of the story, setting, or character?
- Does the primary source draw students into the story or reveal related aspects to the story, increasing engagement?
- Does the primary source enhance aspects of the larger story, setting, or character not shown in the picture book?
- Does the primary source provide context that the story does not, allowing for a richer connection from story to time period, event, or person?

If used with younger students, a primary source image of Nell Richardson and Alice Burke may be analyzed by students prior to the story (Figure 4.5). Using the See, Think, Wonder strategy from Chapter 2, students can anticipate what may be happening in the photo. While they likely will not anticipate the women's suffrage connection, they can determine that there is a sense of celebration for the women and those attending. Analyzing a primary source photo prior to reading an illustrated picture book may also make the story more real for students, allowing them to connect drawn illustrations to photos of the actual people in the story.

A teacher may also look at primary sources connected with literature through the lens of an illustrator. Artistic interpretation of an event through storytelling can be examined as a part of visual literacy. How that imagery enhances elements

Figure 4.5
Miss Richardson and Mrs. A. S. Burke.

of storytelling can be a powerful discussion. Visual literacy may also be used as students analyze a primary source image. Textual descriptions in primary sources can also connect to illustrations in literature. Visual elements such as clothing or technology also help students place the event in a time period. The teacher may consider elements related to the following:

- Visual context in time and place
- Illustrative storytelling
- Illustrative inspiration

The use of primary sources, when viewed through the eyes of the illustrator, can point out inspiration in any of the aforementioned areas. While an illustrator can draw from the author's text in historically focused nonfiction picture book, he or she may also find elements in primary sources that inspire the illustrations. While viewing primary sources through an illustrator's lens, a teacher may ask the following questions:

- Is there any noticeable imagery that may have inspired illustrations that accompany the literature?
- If color is in the primary source image or written of in the text, does it also play a role in the illustration?
- Are there moments written about in primary source text that are illustrated in the book? Do these illustrations seem to draw from primary source text as well as the text in the picture book?
- Are there elements of the book illustrations that appear similar to or inspired by primary source images or text descriptions?

Using primary source photographs and news stories, students can explore the picture book illustrations in our example. Looking for evidence that the illustrator explored primary sources, students can look for visual scenes that look similar and for elements of the characters—including the car—that may have been inspired by primary sources. The same can be done with primary source text by exploring illustrated scenes from the story that were described in a newspaper article. Artistic choices such as medium used or color may also be considered when comparing the book illustrations to primary sources.

A teacher may choose a different photograph than one that would be selected to introduce the book. This photo shows the full car and a wider angle of the festivities around it (Figure 4.6). It may make a better choice because it gives students more to compare when looking at the illustrator's work. Students will likely find a page from early in the book that reminds them of this photo. They can be encouraged to look more carefully at elements of the photo that were taken and used throughout the book. Are there specific aspects of characters or setting in the story that the illustrator has included in the work? Are there elements that have been left

Figure 4.6
Golden Flyer Leaving N.Y. 4/6/16.

out? Since it is a black-and-white photo, how can this be paired with illustrative text that describes color to show even more?

There are times when primary sources play a role in book illustrations that are difficult to determine unless the illustrator shares his or her process. An example that can be shared with elementary students is well documented by illustrator Alice Ratterree for her illustrations in *Dangerous Jane* written by Suzanne Slade. This story of Jane Addams focuses on her life in the late 19th and early 20th centuries. Ratterree shares her exploration of the poverty and working conditions for children of the time shown through the photographs of Jacob Riis and Lewis Hine. The illustrator even shares her exploration of Jane Addams's Hull House and being inspired by the colors and architecture. The account paints an excellent picture of how illustrators can be inspired by primary sources (http://www.aliceink.com/illustrating-nonfiction-jane-addams/).

Finally, when incorporating primary sources into language arts, the teacher may look through an author's lens when selecting primary sources to share with students for analysis. Looking through that lens can give insight into the process an author may have gone through to learn about the topic that would become the focus of a book. While that can sometimes be read through author's notes that accompany a picture book, looking directly at primary sources allows students to bypass the author's explanation of the experience and reproduce aspects of it. This can give students a unique perspective when evaluating the literature and decisions the author made. As a teacher identifies primary sources that may be analyzed by students when looking through the lens of the author, he or she may consider how the author may have:

- Identified the story in the sources
- Defined the character through the sources
- Chose moments to highlight or moments to leave out

The teacher may want to highlight a certain aspect of the writing process. Elementary students often write about what they know. The same can be said of an author who writes about a historical event or an individual, but to know them, the author must learn about it, and primary sources are an avenue to that learning. Depending on what part of the learning and writing process the teacher wants to explore through the picture book, he or she may ask the following questions:

- How can my students reproduce the discovery process the author may have gone through while searching for primary sources?

Pairing primary sources and picture books can give insight into the Author's writing process.

- How may the author have viewed or read the primary source to come to an understanding of the characters in the story?
- How are character traits evident in the primary source?
- Does the primary source highlight an aspect of the story that is noteworthy for an author?

In this case, the students can explore the author's process in several ways. They can identify story points in the picture book chosen by Mara Rockliff and try to identify the same moments mentioned in the primary sources. Were the moments accurately portrayed in the book? Why might the author have chosen to include this moment? What did she appear to have left out? Would you have made a different choice?

One moment from the story can be found in the April 23, 1916, *New-York Tribune* article by Alice Burke herself (Figure 4.7). The diary style report tells of the schoolyard visit that is also written about in the book. It is a perfect opportunity for students to examine a specific account and how it is represented in literature while also exploring other accounts that were not selected to be part of the story of this event.

Students may also read the picture book and identify character traits that were implied by the author's text along with supporting text to support their trait choice. In our example, students can then explore the primary sources and see how the women and their trip were written about. Going through the same process, they can identify character traits for Nell and Alice along with supporting text. Were there similar character traits? If similar or different, why were the women being portrayed this way in the picture book or news story?

Finally, students can replicate the exploration for primary sources that the author may have gone through. After reading the story, students can brainstorm a set of search criteria to use in Chronicling America. Using specific keywords and searching

Figure 4.7
April 23, 1916, *New-York Tribune*.

Richmond, Va., April 12.—We've had women audiences and men crowds around the "Golden Flier," but this morning in little Spotsylvania we were welcomed by 400 school children. They received a special recess when we pulled in, and though we really shouldn't have stopped for anything but a much needed drink of water from the old town pump, yet they clamored so, those 400 dancing, prancing young Americans, that we couldn't refuse. When we had finished we could hardly

Students can identify character traits in a story that connect with an author's writing.

by date may be ideas that surface as they learn the search features of the newspaper database. Found articles can then help students refine their search as they collaboratively create their own curated set of sources that are tied to the event.

There are other primary sources that are connected with literature that tie directly back to the lens of the author or illustrator. Authors and illustrators have interviews, blogs, author visits that have been captured on video, and various other medium that are widely available online. While these do not connect back to specific subject matter, they do allow teacher and students to look through the lens of the author or illustrator to understand aspects of their approach to creating the final work, their struggles, and what they value. These pieces, when considering the creation of books as a topic, become a valued primary source. The person who is sharing is directly connected to the topic and the moment when the creation happened. These types of primary sources allow students and teachers to go well beyond the type of books that are set during a historical time period stretching into fiction set in present day, fantasy, informational nonfiction, and more.

Maybe a class already accesses these types of resources but does not consider them primary sources. What if students did? They could analyze a recorded author's talk much as they would an oral history. They could perform a Close Reading analysis on a transcript of a Q&A for the illustrator of a book. These

Students can search a newspaper database to replicate an author's experience.

approaches can engage elementary students and help them relate to others as writers and artists. While some may argue that it takes the fun out of listening to a person who creates a book, another may argue that it helps students appreciate and understand the work that the author or illustrator puts into his or her craft.

If a teacher and students are lucky enough to host an author or illustrator visit, hear that person at a local bookstore or public library, or reach out to an author or illustrator over social media, consider that individual a primary source. If viewing a photographic primary source, to help students generate questions, a teacher may ask, "What would you ask the person in the photo?" The teacher should consider asking the same thing when preparing students to ask questions. It does require on-the-spot analysis, but students practiced in primary source analysis may discover more depth to their questions when approaching authors and illustrators in this way.

Primary Sources and Science

It may seem unusual to bring historically based primary sources into a science classroom, but when viewing some primary sources, there may be an argument to be made. Science does not sit isolated from the rest of the world. Often, science advances and scientists explore new ideas because of a problem in society or to positively impact society. Primary sources allow us to explore the historical moments where those advances have been made. These moments of primary source analysis can enhance science instruction because they give the science purpose.

One lens a teacher may look through when considering primary sources in science is the lens of an engineer. Goals around thinking scientifically, identifying and exploring problems that have explorable explanations and testable solutions, can be paired with primary sources that reveal a historically real-world problem. The teacher may want to look at overall questions:

- What engineering problem is presented through the primary source?
- Is the problem one that students can investigate and design solutions for?
- What information is shared to understand the problem, and how it impacts individuals?
- What possible solutions are offered?

One element that is an identifiable problem in the news stories of the trip across the United States is the condition of the roads. Roads are described frequently and vary widely. They also have an impact on the individuals, causing damage to their car and delaying their trip. Students have enough awareness of roads today to have an idea of different types of roads, giving them a background they can draw on when exploring the historical problem. When searching for sources that may be used to explore road conditions in the early 1900s, a teacher may ask himself or herself the following questions:

- How does the source help readers visualize the problem of road conditions?
- How does the source clearly show the human impact of the identified problem of road conditions?
- Does the source give insight into solutions to the problem or examples of road conditions that were preferable?
- Does the source or do multiple sources give insight into where the problem of road conditions was most prevalent during the time period?

An April 17, 1916, *New-York Tribune* article from Alice Burke herself gives one account of road troubles (Figure 4.8). The roads not only are full of bumps and ruts but also run through streams. At one point this results in the travelers being stuck in a stream and mud road overnight.

This primary source analysis can connect with other learning by upper-elementary students actually going through the process of identifying the parameters of the problem as well as the human impact and identifying and testing solutions. Students could likely find a place outside to test the conditions of dirt and gravel roads and the impact a vehicle, possibly a bicycle, has on the surfaces by driving on a small piece of them in different conditions. They can push their thinking by exploring

Figure 4.8
April 17, 1916, *New-York Tribune*.

> **Flier Strikes Bad Roads.**
>
> Fredericksburg, Md., April 10 — We left Washington yesterday to do battle with some of the worst roads in the United States. The poor little Flier hopped around from bump to hole, to creek, to rut, to stream, fairly a-bob every minute. Once we got stuck in the bottom of a stream, really stuck so that we couldn't budge. As she sank deeper and deeper in the sand, and the water kept coming up higher and higher, we became worried and jumped into the stream—icy cold because it comes from springs above—and cranked and cranked and cranked our arms nearly off.
>
> "Votes for women," said Miss Richardson, by way of cheer, while I cranked.
>
> "I believe I'll join the good roads campaign, instead." I answered grimly.

likely solutions of the time as primary sources are paired with secondary source information on early road conditions, improvements, and tools from the Smithsonian (http://amhistory.si.edu/onthemove/exhibition/exhibition_8_3.html). The circular idea of identifying a problem, gathering information, designing a solution, and testing can be enhanced through the analysis of primary sources.

While this set of sources may not lend itself to explore a variety of elementary scientific topics, other primary sources do. Some primary source sets have been built including a set on weather forecasting (https://www.loc.gov/teachers/classroommaterials/primarysourcesets/weather-forecasting/) and another with sources exploring scientific data and how scientists recorded observations and shared information (https://www.loc.gov/teachers/classroommaterials/primarysourcesets/scientific-data/). Regardless of the scientific topic, if there is a benefit to exploring in the impact of science and scientific thinking, looking through the lens of a scientific discipline may help determine what role primary sources may play in the student learning.

Primary Sources and Math

Like science, incorporating primary sources into math instruction encourages a look at a real-world and historical perspective to identify and solve problems. These may mimic skills practiced in solving math word problems at other points during the year. Other primary sources may deal with data collection or representing numeric data. Both of the primary source sets in the previous paragraph contain sources with numeric data. In working with this set of primary sources, the teacher may be interested in the following objectives:

- Problem solving involving measurement and estimation
- Representing and interpreting data
- Determining and converting measurement

Looking specifically at these resources, the teacher may search for newspaper articles that talk about distance and time to use with upper-elementary students. There may be a need to also estimate if points and time are mentioned, but not specific distances. These can be looked up using secondary sources; while roads taken may have changed, this can give an example of the messiness of primary sources as well as math that is typically not seen in a classroom. The teacher may ask the following questions:

- Where is distance mentioned or implied by traveling between two points?
- How is the time traveled related to distance in a primary source?
- What other numeric data are revealed or implied through the source?

If students are practicing to create word problems using basic operations, such as addition, subtraction, multiplication, and division, these sources can be used as inspiration for the problems. While the event has long passed, it does provide a real event where there is missing information. Students can find average speeds using distance and time and estimate travel times for unknown information. Breakdowns and unknown road conditions create unknown elements. Students can justify answers on the basis of known information, putting the math into an even richer context.

One possible connection is to return to the diary entries of Alice Burke that are posted in the *New-York Tribune*. In the May 2, 1916, story, Burke provides dates and locations, traveling from Athens to Stone Mountain to Atlanta on April 18, 19, and 20 (Figure 4.9). Students can partner math and geography skills, finding distances and estimating a travel time given a speed of 15 miles per hour, a fair guess given road conditions at the time. A quick search on Chronicling America for the Saxon will give additional information such as average miles per gallon, giving students other factors to consider into their word problems.

Many teachers will begin their primary source integration with social studies. It is such a natural fit that many teachers will feel most comfortable with pairing primary sources directly with history. Look for a place where additional resources would help student learning and visualize what type of primary sources may be available for that topic of study. That may be all that is needed to begin the search. What is found does not need to fit into multiple subject areas like the examples mentioned earlier.

Figure 4.9
May 2, 1916, *New-York Tribune.*

> Stone Mountain, April 19. We've stopped here for luncheon and a rest by the wayside. Miss Richardson is finishing up a dress she started in Pennsylvania, for it will be two hours before we need to start for Decatur, where the Atlanta suffragists are to meet us. Stone Mountain is an interesting geological structure, a single enormous bowlder, perpendicular and 1,000 feet high. The Daughters of the Confederacy propose to cut a great hall out of the stone, setting up figures of some of the greatest Southern heroes. Gutzon Borglum has been engaged to execute this remarkable piece of work, and the undertaking will cost $2,000,000.
>
> Atlanta, April 20.—The Atlanta women gave us a wonderful surprise party, coming with fifteen cars to Decatur and simply crowding the old courthouse steps to greet us. The wife

You do not need to use primary sources in all subject areas. The point is that you can. As you continue to see connections in one subject, be open to thinking about others. Incorporating primary sources into different learning will help that openness, encouraging you to think about other subjects. To help you, as you come across more and more primary sources in your searching, continue to look at them through different subject area lenses. Pairings of primary sources and subject areas will begin to reveal themselves.

Chapter 5

Assuring Success with Primary Source Analysis: Teacher Tips

For students' primary source analysis to be successful, it is essential that they use a clear primary-source-analysis strategy on a meaningful primary source that relates to past or future learning. This has been the focus of Chapters 2, 3, and 4. I already mentioned that my first attempts at doing this were not as successful as I had hoped. It was not because I had a bad primary source, a flawed primary-source-analysis strategy, or lacked connection to other learning. The reason the lesson was less than I had hoped for was because of many small things that make a difference in primary source analysis.

I began asking myself questions that I did not always have clear answers to. Why might I choose one primary source over another when they are very similar? When I am connecting primary source analysis to other learning, when is the best time to bring the primary source analysis into the lesson? How do I balance students learning from each other and giving each student a chance to contribute during a primary source analysis? How can I facilitate a primary source analysis and encourage students to take ownership of their own learning and be engaged?

I think these are important questions. They were questions that I sought out answers to by reflecting on my teaching and my students' work when they interacted with primary sources. What I discovered was that these small but important decisions that impact a student's primary source analysis were all things I had control over but were also things I did not always know how to control. Some of them changed how I looked at primary sources. Others changed how I looked at my own instruction. Still others shifted how I saw students as learners.

I have no doubt that you can discover these answers on your own or find your own answer to a similar question. You may already have some of these mastered through other teaching. My hope is that by sharing them, you will spend less time trying to answer the questions for yourself and more time moving toward facilitating great primary source analyses with your students.

Collaborative Classroom Culture during Primary Source Analysis

This may be an area where many elementary educators already excel. Collaborative learning is a staple in many classrooms. As a teacher is beginning primary source analysis, the focus may be on his or her teaching moves and not student interactions. There are dynamic benefits to students analyzing collaboratively. Consider the many options for collaboration that students have during the analysis process. Exploring these options initially may seem overwhelming. Instead, a teacher may continue to use collaboration configurations that are used in other student learning. As students begin to show their thinking and learning during primary source analysis, the teacher may want to look at other forms of collaboration to support students and push that thinking even further.

Collaboration Configurations during Primary Source Analysis

Whole-Class Collaboration

This is the most common type of collaboration during primary source analysis, especially with the youngest learners and as students are using a new strategy or are analyzing a new format of primary source. Whole-class analysis gives the teacher an opportunity to hear all offerings from students and model parts of the analysis process by documenting and organizing students' thinking, demonstrating think alouds and helping students clarify their thinking. From a student's perspective, whole-class collaboration gives that student a safe space to listen to others' thinking when unsure of his or her own. It also allows a student to participate in the part of the analysis process where he or she is more uncomfortable and to listen and learn during other parts of the process. Finally, it gives a student a variety of perspectives to hear, which can encourage him or her to view and think about the primary source differently. One drawback includes the limited amount of participation any one student can give during the time allowed for a primary source analysis.

Small-Group Collaboration

Collaborating in groups of three or four students is another way to provide student support from their peers as they go through the primary-source-analysis process. As students become more familiar with a primary-source-analysis strategy, even younger learners can collaborate in small groups. While the teacher cannot hear every idea shared in the groups, he or she can rotate through all of the groups to hear parts of the analysis process. At the end of the process, the teacher may also recount what was heard in different groups in a whole-class discussion or call on all groups to share a part of their thinking with the whole class. For a student,

Students can work in small groups after they are familiar with an analysis strategy.

small-group collaboration gives more of an opportunity to voice observations, reactions, or questions. While not often stated, there is more of an expectation within the group for everyone to contribute to the task. There is still safe space though for the student to listen to others when he or she is not sure what to offer during parts of the analysis process. Drawbacks may come when several students within a group are unsure of the same part of the analysis process. Students having prior experiences with the primary-source-analysis strategy can help. In addition, organizers to document their own thinking and the teachers providing transition points or check-ins may help alleviate this potential problem.

Pair Collaboration

As students become more familiar with analysis or even part of an analysis strategy, pairing students for the process makes sense. Especially when working with a trusted partner, working in pairs gives students the safest place to take risks during primary source analysis. Those students who are observers during whole-class or small-group settings can suddenly find their voice when working with one partner. Like small-group settings, organizers and teacher transitions can help guide students during paired analysis. Reminding students of language used

Working in pairs can be a safe place to take risks.

during a primary source analysis such as "I see, I think, I wonder" can also be helpful to encourage conversation. A teacher may have an opportunity to listen to small parts of several collaborations during this time. Because of the number of simultaneous conversations, the teacher may target his or her attention on specific pairs of students who may need support. This may also give the teacher the opportunity to share small modelings with a pair of students. If students are struggling with a part of the process, he or she may share, "I heard another pair of students making the same observation that I see you made. It helped them focus their attention on this part of the photo. You might want to focus there and see what seems important." A drawback to paired collaborations can include students not hearing as many perspectives. A teacher giving pairs a chance to share part of their thinking at moments during the analysis can help alleviate that concern.

Mixing Collaborations during Primary Source Analysis

Primary-source-analysis strategies have different steps. Each one of those steps can be an opportunity to vary the type of collaboration students are participating in. More experienced students, even younger learners, may have a small part of the analysis process where they are working individually and then come together to share and collaborate. One advantage of varying the collaboration is that it helps to keep the primary-source-analysis strategy feeling new and different for students. While it is beneficial for students to feel comfortable with the steps in the strategy, varying how those steps are approached will stop students from feeling they are repeating the same task again and again. Another advantage is the continual move toward students independently analyzing primary sources. Having several different moments where students can practice this still is important but so is the support that a teacher provides in guiding them toward independent analysis. An elementary student may never independently analyze a primary source from beginning to end, but a teacher may feel comfortable, after students have used a strategy, in independently working through part of an analysis. Coming back together collaboratively in different ways gives the teacher and the students an opportunity to check-in to confirm and broaden their thinking.

Collaboration as a Way to Address Student Misconceptions

One of the main benefits to primary source analysis is that elementary students become engaged in the process and through that engagement take ownership of their own thinking. A drawback, though, is that limited experiences as a young person, along with misconceptions that students bring to their learning, can stifle or derail the primary-source-analysis process. Collaboration helps to buffer that. Hearing the observations of other students fills in gaps that all students can bring to their learning. Shared observations, reflections, and questions help students look at a primary source in a new way and expand their analysis.

Misconceptions can still arise. When students voice misconceptions as they analyze a primary source, there may be a small number of students that agree with that misconception, but more often there are students that provide alternatives. Having a supportive, collaborative environment encourages students to be open to acknowledging those misconceptions and breaking them down.

Even when misconceptions persist, the teacher does not need to directly correct the student. Instead, he or she can lead even younger elementary students collaboratively through a historical thinking process.

I once had a librarian contact me about a primary source photo of children dressed up for a Thanksgiving celebration and a misconception that took place (Figure 5.1). She asked, "What do you do when one misguided idea hijacks the discussion?" Here, one student surmised, because the boy on the right is holding a toy gun, that he and the other *boys* were robbing the *girl*. The misconception, on the basis of an observation, took over the talk in the library. How could she get it back to other observations, reactions, and questions so that she could teach about the Thanksgiving tradition shown in the photograph?

Figure 5.1
Thanksgiving.

THANKSGIVING

When one insistent student holds on to a misconception, I do one of a few things. If it is a comment that comes and goes and no one else reacts to it, we just document it and move on. These are fairly easy because the misconception dies on the vine.

When the student continues to repeat his or her interpretation or other students pick it up and build on it as if it is a fact, we stop and have a lesson in thinking like historians. In this case, I suggested that we first acknowledge that we think the person on the right is robbing the other people. This is our idea. Second, we see what the idea is based on. While the student may offer an entire story of what is happening, in this case, it came down to the toy gun in the photo.

This is where we stop and think like historians. We look for other evidence that supports the idea of a robbery. Students may point to other people standing around. And we look for evidence that tells us it may not be a robbery. In this case, if students don't see any evidence, I would suggest thinking about how people would be feeling if they were robbing someone or if they were being robbed. If they felt a certain way, how would they look? Now compare that to what you see in the photo. Here we have people standing and smiling, leaning against a ledge. No one seems alarmed or afraid. Even the person (who I believe is a boy) in the skirt shows a smile behind the covered face.

Finally, we look at where we have more evidence. Hopefully students will have more evidence that this isn't a robbery; disregard the misconception; and now be open to making new observations, reflections, and questions. As students work to base their interpretations of a moment on multiple observations, misconceptions can be set aside.

Considering Moment of Use

There are a number of teachers who use primary source analysis as a bell ringer activity, a short activity that students can do, usually independently, as they come into the classroom. There may be a place for these types of activities when it comes to primary sources after students are familiar with an analysis strategy and are able to work independently. With the time that primary source analysis can take at an elementary level and the amount of support and collaborative interaction needed for a successful analysis, primary source analysis may be better placed within instruction with elementary students. Other related activities such as reading others' handwriting or writing with the long S (see Chapter 3) may be better choices for bell ringer activities related to primary source analysis.

When considering a primary source, strategy, and connection to curriculum, it can also be helpful to anticipate when the primary source will be used within other learning. Factors such as time allowed, students' background knowledge, level of independent work, and what the purpose for the primary source analysis is can hinge on when that analysis takes place in the learning. Let's return to the Statue of Liberty example from Chapter 2. If considering using a primary source during a lesson on the history of the Statue of Liberty, when might certain primary sources and primary-source-analysis strategies be used?

Primary Sources at the Beginning of a Lesson

If looking for a primary source for the beginning of the lesson, as stated in Chapter 2, a teacher might select the photo of Bartholdi's warehouse workshop. A teacher may be looking for a primary source that:

- Is visual and allows students little hurdles to begin interacting with the source
- Provides some familiar aspects to connect with students' prior knowledge as well as likely unknown elements that encourage students to look closely
- Allow students to react to the primary source, revealing background knowledge that they have
- Encourages students to ask questions, making them want to know more

The Bartholdi's warehouse workshop photo does all of these things. The statue head and arm are familiar. Students who know something of the

Analyzing a primary source at the beginning of a lesson encourages students to ask questions.

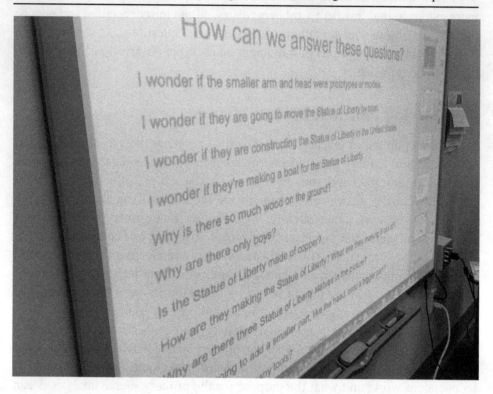

construction of the statue have an opportunity to react, giving the teacher an understanding of any background knowledge on this topic. There are a number of details and places to look in the photo, giving students many entry points to engage. Most important, those entry points are also opportunities for students to ask questions, something that teachers often want when using a primary source at the beginning of the lesson.

This type of primary source pairs nicely with a See, Wonder, Think strategy that directs students' attention on questions that arise from observations. Other strategies or modified strategies that have students voicing questions as part of the analysis can also be used. Whole-class or small-group collaboration that shares back with the entire class can allow the teacher to gather as many questions as possible to use as a motivation for upcoming learning in the lesson.

Primary Sources as Part of Whole-Class Instruction

Another place to bring primary sources into the lesson is during whole-class instruction. This can be the most supported moment of primary source analysis. Students likely have some background knowledge from earlier in the lesson, and a student can draw from other students' observations, reactions, and questions.

There is a cumulative understanding that can come from primary source analysis in this moment that can pull a class together. This is also supported by the teacher who hears every voiced part of the analysis and can encourage students to clarify their thinking, facilitate discussion during the analysis, and model, if necessary. Because of all of this support, a teacher may seek out a primary source that:

- Is more complex than the typical primary source students have used
- Builds upon prior knowledge or experiences the teacher knows all students have
- Is a new format of primary source that may require some modeling
- May uncover misconceptions that the teacher suspects some in the class have

Continuing learning about the construction of the Statue of Liberty, a teacher could select an 1878 article from the *Forest Republican* titled "The Statue for New York Harbor" (Figure 5.2). It gives an account from a French newspaper of where the building of the statue is at the moment, sharing that the arm holding the torch is already in the United States.

If students are less familiar with analyzing primary source newspapers or a close reading strategy that may accompany it, this may be a reason to bring the piece into whole-class instruction. Depending on the age of students using it, the article could be considered long, and elements of the article—possibly because it is translated from a French newspaper article—may be confusing to students. Analyzing it as a class gives the teacher an opportunity to carefully see how the analysis unfolds and step in if misconceptions are arising.

The piece may also be considered a building piece on previous learning. If the students analyzed the photograph of the workshop, this piece that references Bartholdi's workshop and some of the work happening within it may reveal answers to earlier questions.

Primary Sources during Independent Instruction

During a lesson, students are likely to work independently on part of their learning. As elementary students continue their exploration of the Statue of Liberty, the teacher may choose an 1876 stereograph card of the arm and torch of the Statue of Liberty on display in Philadelphia (Figure 5.3). In searching for a primary source for students to analyze independently, a teacher may be looking for the following:

- A primary source format that students are familiar with
- A source with clear connections to previous learning that students can draw upon
- The pairing of two simple primary sources that inform each other

Figure 5.2
April 17, 1878, *Forest Republican.*

The Statue for New York Harbor.

A French paper says : The colossal statue of "Liberty Lighting the World," erected by France and America in remembrance of their old friendship, is coming out little by little from the immense workshops established expressly for its construction in the Rue de Chazelles, No. 25, near Monceaux Park. The arm and hand holding the torch are already in America, and at present the sculptor, Bartholdi, is finishing the principal portion of the head. The plaster model is nearly completed. In a few days it will be stripped of the scaffolding which surrounds it and upon which several gangs of men are at work. The first sentiment inspired by the enormous head, nearly thirty feet high, is almost terror. Its gigantic dimensions are stupefying; but by degrees the eye becomes accustomed to the colossal forms, and the mind reconciles itself to the extent of those great lines, and we discover in the midst of them the majesty and the light which the author has endeavored to give to the features. But the public will soon have an opportunity to see the beauty of this work, for the head of the statue of Liberty is to be exhibited at the Universal Exposition. Nevertheless, we strongly advise every one beforehand to visit the establishment on the Rue de Chazelles and see how the different portions of this head are prepared, worked and adjusted. M. Bartholdi is making copies in plaster of his statue of Liberty. Two hundred of them only will be executed, numbered and registered with the name of the purchaser, who may in this may preserve a souvenir of this magnificent commemorative of the centennial anniversary of the independence of the United States, and destined to renew and enliven the old friendship between France and America.

Figure 5.3
Colossal Hand and Torch "Liberty".

Like the newspaper article, the photo of the statue's arm and torch is connected to prior learning. The image not only gives a visual to a reference in the earlier newspaper article but also provides details that were not given. This allows students to focus on something familiar and find new information within it.

Using a See, Think, Wonder strategy or another analysis strategy that students are very familiar with gives them the ability to do much of the analysis on their own. The teacher will likely have moments during the analysis where students can check in with a partner or small group to assure some support. Including moments of support as well as interacting with familiar formats and strategies can help guarantee students success when working more independently during primary source analysis. While not done here, primary sources can also be paired to support each other. More will be explored later in this chapter about advantages to pairing primary sources.

Primary Sources Analysis as Assessment

Similar to using a primary source during independent learning, primary sources used as part of an assessment should lend themselves to be analyzed independently depending on the type of assessment a teacher wants to do. Familiar primary source formats and analysis strategies should be priorities when making decisions about assessment.

Analyzing a primary source as part of an assessment can reveal not only what a student knows but also how the student thinks about an event or an individual. The assessment analysis should be framed by the teacher just like any other primary source analysis, allowing the teacher to focus a student's attention while still knowing that a student may not speak directly to what a teacher is expecting them to when analyzing the source. This is the main reason that what is assessed is the student's process of analysis. If the teacher is interested in what a student knows concerning specific facts, primary source analysis may not be the best choice.

When selecting a primary source to be used for analysis, a teacher may look for a primary source:

- Previously used in instruction that can be framed in a different way
- From a related topic to compare with the event or person under study
- That clearly represents a perspective on the topic of study
- Connected to previous learning or previously analyzed primary sources

Returning to the lesson, the teacher may return to the original Bartholdi's workshop photo (Figure 5.4). It is not only a familiar image but also a format that students are comfortable with. The teacher can choose the Jump In strategy if it is one that students are familiar with. Framing the analysis, he or she may ask students to take their previous learning and jump into the photo to become one of the workers. The teacher may ask them to describe what is happening in the photo to the photographer, Albert Fernique. While this does allow the teacher to assess content

Figure 5.4
Workmen Constructing the Statue of Liberty in Bartholdi's Parisian Warehouse Workshop.

knowledge, observing where the students focus their attention in the photo as well as how they react to those observations allows the teacher to also assess the process the students go through when analyzing the source.

Listening and Responding during Primary Source Analysis

I believe this is the most challenging aspect to facilitating a primary source analysis. Teachers often want to talk and share information. Teachers want to react and confirm to build upon what students are saying. What may be helpful to think about is that a primary source analysis is a thinking process where thinking is expressed aloud and evolves as students hear and see new information. How a teacher responds to that thinking impacts how that thinking process evolves.

Listening during a Primary Source Analysis

Before a student begins to share, it is important for the teacher to be familiar with the primary source that the student is working with. This typically is not a problem if the teacher selected the source. If students are finding their own sources, selecting from a group of sources, or the primary-source-analysis activity was not put together by that teacher, he or she should take some time to become familiar with the source. This may be as quick as looking or reading over the source briefly or as long as walking through the possible analysis. Either of them will help the teacher understand and even anticipate what the student is trying to communicate.

During a whole-class primary source analysis or when talking with a student about his or her primary source analysis, the teacher will be listening for the following:

- An observation, reaction, or question from the student
- Evidence that what the student is analyzing stays within how the teacher framed the analysis
- Proof of understanding or misconception
- Connections to other parts of the analysis
- Potential for future connections and learning

That is a lot to listen for, and all of these can be found in a single student's statement. Remember that in a whole-class primary source analysis, there will be dozens of statements made. It is no wonder that listening is so important but also so challenging.

Why are all of these listen-fors important? They all help the teacher decide how to react to the student statement. The student should be making an observation, reaction, or question directly connected to the source. Many teachers have had someone similar to the young elementary student who, during a discussion of the Statue of Liberty, decides to share the story of her family's trip to New York. This is an obvious example where the student goes outside the focus of the analysis. More likely, though, as a student is giving one of these three responses, the teacher will be documenting and modeling. The teacher has also framed the analysis. If the student's statement, even if it is about the primary source, seems to be outside of what the focus of the analysis is, the teacher may intervene. A student's statement may also give some insight into the student's thinking. Is he or she using prior knowledge to connect to other understandings? Are those understandings correct, or is there an evidence of a misconception? Connections may also be within the analysis itself. The student's sharing may be connected to an earlier observation, reaction, or question that the student or another student shared. Finally, the teacher may anticipate what future learning this analysis is connected to. An observation, reaction, or question that a student makes may be part of a bridge from analysis to future learning.

As the teacher listens, small clues will be given to help make the link between what the student is saying and what the teacher is listening for. Let's examine a small part of a primary source analysis to get a better understanding. We will revisit the primary source analysis written about earlier in the chapter that contained a student misconception.

A teacher wants students to study traditions throughout the school year. In November, a primary source photo is brought to students. Framing the analysis, he or she tells them that most families have traditions around holidays like Thanksgiving, but traditions sometimes do not last forever and that students will be studying a lost tradition. The teacher shares that their analysis will be a first step in uncovering the mystery of that lost tradition.

What the teacher knows about the source but does not tell the students is that the photo is showing the tradition of Thanksgiving Maskers. The predominantly New York tradition took place in the early to mid-20th century. Children and, sometimes, adults would dress up on Thanksgiving Day, parade through the streets, and knock on doors asking for candy or pennies.

Sharing the primary source photo, the teacher asks students to start sharing their observations. Students offer the following:

Student 1: "I see four people."
Student 2: "I see five. There's someone inside."
Student 3: "They're dressed funny."
Student 4: "They have on weird hats and makeup on their face."
Student 3: "I think they might be clowns."
Student 5: "There are signs on the window."
Student 6: "That kid looks like a scarecrow." Points to person outside on right.
Student 7: "He is holding a gun."
Student 6: "He's a robber."
Student 7: "I think those three guys are robbing that girl."

Earlier in the chapter, it is clear that the sharing from students goes beyond this exchange. The idea that the photo is of a group of men robbing a woman overtakes the conversation. Let's look at the beginning of this exchange to see what a teacher hears as students share their analysis.

Student 1: "I see four people."
Student 1's statement is an observation. It is connected to the framing of the analysis because those are the people that the teacher wants the students to focus on. Since this is the beginning of the analysis and this is a basic observation, there is little else to find in this first statement.

Student 2: "I see five. There's someone inside."
The next student's statement is also an observation. The fifth person in the photo is not important to what the teacher wants students to uncover, but there is no way for the student to know this. It is connected back to the first student's observation.

Student 3: "They're dressed funny."
This student is reacting to an observation that he hasn't voiced yet. There are observations that have not been shared yet about the way the four people are dressed, which he thinks, is funny. The way the people in the photo are dressed is connected to the framing of the analysis and will connect to additional learning after the analysis.

Student 4: "They have on weird hats and makeup on their face."
Student 4 is making observations connected to the reaction that Student 3 just shared. It is also within the framing of the analysis and can also connect to future learning.

Student 3: "I think they might be clowns."
Student 3 shares another reaction, this time being more specific about what he thinks he is seeing in the photo. While connected to the previous sharings, it could lead to a misconception about what is happening in the photo.

Student 5: "There are signs on the window."
This student shares an observation about the signs seen in the window. The student does not share what is written on the signs. Her observation may encourage someone else to share that information. This observation does not have a direct connection to earlier statements or directly connect to the framing of the analysis.

Student 6: "That kid looks like a scarecrow." Points to person outside on right.
Student 6 shares a reaction that some may see as an observation. There is something specific that she sees in that person in the photograph that reminds her of a

scarecrow, but it is not clear what it is. It does connect back to earlier observations and reactions about the people standing in front of the window, and since it is about their attire, it will connect to future learning.

Student 7: "He is holding a gun."
Student 7 makes an observation that is connected back to the previous reaction. He has likely looked more closely at this person in the photo in reaction to Student 6 describing him as a scarecrow. That led to this new observation. While possibly connected to future learning, the observation of a gun feels very out of context with what was said earlier. Because of that, the teacher may feel that it could lead to a misconception.

Student 6: "He's a robber."
Student 6 comes back into the conversation with another reaction, this time clearly connecting the previous observation to the idea that the person is a robber. Interestingly, this has no connection to the reaction made seconds earlier that the same person looked like a scarecrow. That disconnect between statements as well as the movement away from what is actually taking place in the photo may lend additional weight to a misconception that may take root.

Student 7: "I think those three guys are robbing that girl."
Student 7 comes back into the conversation with a reaction sharing what he thinks is happening in the photo. Obviously, on the basis of the past two statements, the student begins to build on the single observation and the reaction that followed. Misconceptions are building and being repeated in this statement.

Looking for these points in students' writings is also important. Since many teachers will begin their journey with students' primary source analysis in whole-class situations, this piece focuses on listening. The assumption is that students will be sharing ideas aloud and the teacher will be recording them. As students begin documenting their own primary source analysis, the same things a teacher listens for become things he or she looks for.

Responding during a Primary Source Analysis

Reading through these few student sharings mentioned earlier from a primary source analysis, it is easy to see that misconceptions have the potential to take over the analysis. The teacher is not only listening but he or she also has opportunities to respond to students during the analysis.

Like listening, during a whole-class primary source analysis or when talking with a student about the primary source analysis, the teacher will be responding in certain ways:

- Acknowledging or identifying an observation, reaction, or question
- Asking for clarification
- Modeling thinking
- Asking for a connection to an observation, reaction, question, or the framing of the analysis
- Addressing a misconception

These types of responses are important because they help to support a student's thinking during the primary source analysis. Several responses ask for clarification or assist the student in expressing his or her thinking during the analysis. The teacher will often acknowledge a student's sharing with a head nod or by documenting it. As shared when describing the See, Think, Wonder strategy in Chapter 2, affirming or saying one thing is correct may hinder other students' responses. Identifying may simply be pointing out something that a student observes during analysis so that the whole group can see it as well. A teacher may also ask for clarification if unsure what a student is saying. That may look like a teacher asking a student to point out what is being observed or asking the student to restate the reaction or question in a different way. If a student is having trouble verbalizing his or her thinking, the teacher may model that thinking, being sure to ask the student if the modeling is accurate and if he or she would like to add anything. When students make reactions or questions that do not have a clear connection back to an observation, a teacher may ask for students to share their connection. Finally, the teacher can address misconceptions during the primary-source-analysis process if it appears that those misconceptions are taking hold or may be interfering with the success of the analysis within the framework that the teacher has provided.

These are not the only things that a teacher will say during a primary source analysis but they are also typical responses he or she will make to students. The teacher will also frame the analysis and transition from stage to stage during the analysis. See examples for different analysis strategies in Chapter 2.

Let's return to the earlier statements made by students but this time explore likely responses from the teacher.

Student 1: "I see four people."
Knowing that there are five people in the photo, the teacher may ask the student to point them out. Since it is fairly obvious that the student is pointing out the four in the forefront of the photo, the teacher may simply respond by recording the student's observation.

Student 2: "I see five. There's someone inside."
Again, the teacher may simply record the student's observation.

Student 3: "They're dressed funny."
Since the student has not identified what is "funny" about the outfits, the teacher can ask the student to clarify by asking, "What makes you say that?" The teacher can give the student an opportunity to follow up to their own reaction.

Student 4: "They have on weird hats and makeup on their face."
If Student 3 has followed up with observations, these additional observations can be added to the list by the teacher.

Student 3: "I think they might be clowns."
This reaction may be tied to the makeup on the face, but if the teacher wants to confirm, he or she can ask, "Is it the makeup and hats that make you think that?" As students are becoming more adept at primary source analysis, the teacher can push the student to observe more widely. He or she may ask, "Do you see anything in addition to the makeup and hats that make you think they are clowns, or do you see anything that makes you think they might not be clowns?"

Student 5: "There are signs on the window."
Observations are moving in a new direction. The teacher can document the posters to acknowledge the observation. He or she may also count them aloud as the observation is documented.

Student 6: "That kid looks like a scarecrow." Points to person outside on right.
There is again a reaction that is not clearly tied to observations that have been shared. The teacher may react by asking, "What do you see that makes you think that?"

Student 7: "He is holding a gun."
The teacher may simply document this observation.

Student 6: "He's a robber."
This reaction is clearly tied to the previous observation, so there is not a reason to ask what the student sees to make her think that. She has changed her opinion in a matter of seconds though. The teacher may do one of two things. She may document the reaction and move on not wanting to give weight to the statement in the hope that it does not gain traction. If the teacher wants to address the misconception, he or she may ask the student to clarify the two reactions.

"Just a moment ago you said the person was dressed like a scarecrow. Now you shared that you think he is a robber. I see the observations you are making but you are also coming up with more than one possibility for this person and they are very different. Can you put together multiple observations to make a reaction to what this person may be doing?"

Student 7: "I think those three guys are robbing that girl."
At this point, the misconception is starting to build and likely should be addressed before it continues. The teacher can follow the course of action written about earlier in the chapter in the subsection "Collaboration as a Way to Address Student Misconceptions."

Pairing Primary Sources for Student Learning

Primary sources have a mystery to them. They do not state every fact or detail about a topic. This is one thing that can make them compelling. They make us wonder. Sometimes that missing information can be problematic for elementary students. The problem can be the lack of information in the source itself, a lack of background knowledge for the student, or a combination of the two.

Why Pair Primary Sources?

Sometimes primary sources can be made more meaningful to student learning when they are paired together. Pairing together two primary sources may make sense when:

- Viewing multiple perspectives
- One source tells a limited portion of a story and a second source can fill in gaps
- A source does not make sense to most students without another source to give background
- Questions typically asked by one source can be answered by a second source
- Two different formats of primary source reveal similar details in different ways
- One source begins to reveal a topic and the second source builds upon it or extends the understanding of the topic

Pairing Primary Sources with Multiple Perspectives

Every primary source has a perspective. The creator had something that he or she wanted to show. Some perspectives are easy to identify. Letters and political cartoons, for example, often have a clear perspective. Photo primary sources can be more challenging to identify with a perspective. Looking at titles and descriptions from the creator along with the background of that person can be helpful. Observing what is shown and what is not in the photo as well as where the focus of the photo is can also help to reveal perspective.

Figure 5.5
November 24, 1913, *New-York Tribune*.

> But here in New York what greets us
> on this great feast? For many years I
> have been making notes. In this town,
> and in this, I believe, alone, maskers in
> silly, fantastic and often disgusting cos-
> tume parade, straggle along and clog the
> sidewalks. They are oftenest children,
> who waylay the passerby with petitions
> for money, and make the crisp November
> air hideous with tooting horns, beating
> pans and yells. At times adults are the
> mummers. Two years ago this Thanks-
> giving, on walking down Central Park
> West to a late dinner, I saw bands of
> grown boys and men, clothed in the ex-
> ternals of women's garb, roaring and
> tooting in a general saturnalia.

Returning to the Thanksgiving Maskers photo from earlier, what might the perspective be? The Maskers are the focus of the photo. They are smiling and posing.
The woman looking through the window does not seem troubled by them. This
photo seems to have a generally positive perspective of the Maskers. One might
even imagine a parent of these children taking this photo today.

Contrast that with an editorial about Maskers and their activities (Figure 5.5).
The writer of the editorial describes the parade of children as "disgusting" and
the sounds that come from it as "hideous." Quite the opposite perspective is
shared. If this was the only primary source students would interact with, they
would see the tradition as negative and disruptive.

What benefits are there to pairing these primary sources together? It can give
students a richer understanding of not only who Thanksgiving Maskers were but
also what people thought of them.

This does not have to be limited to two perspectives. A teacher may bring in
even more primary sources to illustrate multiple perspectives of a person or event.
There are reasons to limit the number of perspectives. They include time for the
activity and scope of the learning, but as students begin to identify one and two
perspectives, they typically can identify additional perspectives more quickly,
especially if that is the framing of the analysis of the primary source.

Pairing Primary Sources to Fill in the Gaps or Answer Questions

A primary source rarely tells everything about an event. There are often gaps in
information after a primary source analysis. This is why elementary students
being able to ask their own questions is such an important part of many primary-

source-analysis strategies. When there are gaps in understanding or questions posed, a teacher may consider bringing in a second primary source to begin answering those questions.

This is typically done with elementary students beginning with a primary source image or film. A compelling primary source image or film often contains visual details that give some information about an event or person and do not reveal others. Sometimes the title or description, if shared with students, can answer some basic questions, but more complex questions that go beyond that moment the source was captured remain.

Primary source text or audio typically pairs well with the visual primary source to begin to answer students' questions and fill gaps in understanding. This may be a newspaper article, audio interview, or written letter. These sources can give descriptions that go beyond the moment of the visual primary source or explain elements that may have been unclear in the photo or film.

Imagine that a class is studying inventions and inventors. Looking back at key moments, a teacher may bring in the December 17, 1903, photo of the Wright brothers' first flight (Figure 5.6). After an initial look, there is much to observe here. Details of the terrain can be made out. The height of the plane can be estimated. Even parts of the plane itself can be made out in detail when viewing a

Figure 5.6
First Flight, 120 Feet in 12 Seconds 10:35 a.m.; Kitty Hawk, North Carolina.

Figure 5.7
December 17 Diary Entry of Orville Wright.

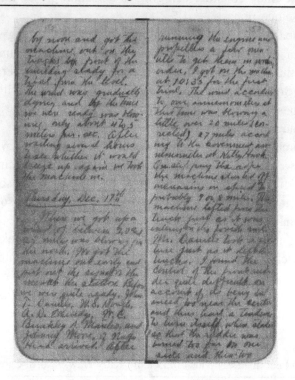

high-definition image. This may lead students to ask questions about what actually happened that day. How many times did they fly? How fast was the plane? What were the weather conditions? What was it like to fly on the plane?

Pairing the photo with Orville Wright's journal from the same day can begin to answer some of those questions (Figure 5.7). Orville documents the wind conditions. He describes why the first flight was only 12 seconds and then gives detailed accounts of the four trips of the day. The details in the journal give students an idea of what that day was like beyond the moment the photo was taken. They also likely answer some questions students will generate from analyzing the photo.

To pair any primary sources together successfully, a teacher wants to anticipate common questions that may arise from the analysis of the first primary source. This is more likely to happen if the teacher frames the primary source analysis to focus the students' attention on an element of the visual primary source and puts himself or herself in the role of the student when selecting the primary source.

Pairing Primary Sources to Reinforce Understandings and Ideas

Sometimes the teacher may want to reinforce understandings gained from an analysis of a primary source. Maybe the information is new or unusual to the students. The teacher may want to show students that what was shown in the primary source was not a one-time event or was not unusual. This may happen when the focus of the analysis does not easily relate to elementary students' everyday lives. It may be focused on an aspect of culture or characteristics of an individual.

Returning to the newspaper advertisements for chocolate and candy from Chapter 2 can give an example of analyzing multiple primary sources to reinforce an understanding or idea. Notice that the new learning, that candy was advertised as a healthy and nutritious choice for children, is something that would not be typical to the world of a child today who is analyzing the source. This unexpected message is an obvious choice to reinforce through multiple primary sources.

Consider possible reactions from students when analyzing just one of these advertisements. There would likely be some who believe there is one candy company, or seller, that has an odd or humorous message about their product. They might even think that the entire message is meant to be a joke to the reader.

Reading more advertisements with the same general message can change the reaction of those students. What once was novelty now appears to be common. This idea of healthy and wholesomeness, even if it was not commonplace, was certainly not unusual during a period of time.

Finding that common element through a second primary source gives reinforcement to the idea that what was found was not unusual for the time period. Similar to focusing on multiple perspectives, additional primary sources can be brought in to continue to solidify the understanding taken from the initial primary source analysis.

Pairing Primary Sources to Extend or Broaden a Topic

A primary source focuses on a topic of study. Its analysis is also connected to other learning. The new learning that comes from a primary source analysis may extend into a related topic or broaden the topic of study that students are examining. This exploration of a second primary source can give students a new perspective on the first primary source.

As a student explores a primary source, questions that the student asks may take him or her away from the topic of study or push it beyond what the teacher anticipated. A teacher has the option of redirecting that student away from the student's questions, but that interest and engagement the student shows could be capitalized on by encouraging the student to explore additional primary sources that can help the student answer those questions.

Returning to Alice Burke and Nell Richardson's trip across the United States, as students read primary sources about the trip, they may discover that one purpose was to drum up support for a silent march by suffragettes at the Democratic and Republican National Conventions. This idea of a silent march may be new to a student, and he or she may inquire what it was and why the suffragettes would do it. While still under the realm of civics, expanding studies into the marches may fall outside what a teacher expected students to explore. Encouraging that exploration should be considered. From our example, it builds upon guiding questions the teacher was exploring in the creation of the original lesson. It is also difficult to discount the benefits of student interest. If that interest can be met through the student working through additional analyses of primary sources, think of the learning that can take place, not only content learning but learning in the skill of primary source analysis as well.

Depending on time, the teacher may even want to encourage the student in seeking out additional primary sources. The hunt to find answers to his or her own questions may add to the student's enthusiasm and satisfaction in finding answers. The teacher can also brainstorm keywords to search and help the student anticipate what he or she hopes to see in the search results.

The student may find the front page of the *Carson City Daily Appeal* from June 14, 1916 (Figure 5.8). The headlines and articles give information about the silent parade in St. Louis, put the number of participants at 5,000, and reveal that delegates to the convention had to walk by all of the suffragettes as they lined the street from the hotel to where the convention was held. These details may be enough to satisfy the curiosity of the student. If more questions arise, additional primary sources or secondary sources could continue to help reveal answers.

Figure 5.8
June 14, 1916, *Carson City Daily Appeal*.

Applause -- Suffragettes, 5000 Strong, Have Silent Parade as Delegates Wind Their Way From Hotel to Place of Meeting

[By United Press]
ST. LOUIS, June 14.—Five thousand suffragists lined the street this morning between the Jefferson hotel and the Coliseum, silently eyeing the delegates enroute to the convention. Their demonstration lasted two hours

speech at 1 o'clock. A Wilson demonstration started at 1.07, in which the New Jersey delegates paraded, and the cheering lasted sixteen minutes.

Glynn smilingly watched the demonstration, his arms folded, and the crowd sang "John Brown's Body." Bryan excitedly waved a flag. The

This pairing of primary sources to expand and build on the topic may concern those who are sensitive to the time constraints in every classroom. These types of journeys, especially those that are student driven, typically last for one or two rounds of questions before students are satisfied and ready to wrap up their primary source investigations. The teacher needs to weigh the benefits of a student having the experience of being an empowered and self-directed learner versus the time it may take from other learning. There are often creative scheduling solutions that have a minimal impact to student learning that a teacher can search for.

An Additional Note on Analyzing Paired Primary Sources

When an elementary student interacts with additional sources looking for evidence of a specific understanding, he or she may not perform a full analysis. That student is likely following all of the same steps, making observations, reacting to the primary source, and asking questions. This time the student may have framed his or her own analysis when searching for the answer to a question or specific information from the source.

As students work collaboratively to analyze additional primary sources, the students will show their comfort level in documenting the primary source analysis. They may ask for the same organizer you typically assign to write down their thinking. They may instead write directly on the sources or even leave out written parts of the process. That does not necessarily mean they are not performing that part of the analysis. It may instead show that students are internalizing the process. Remember that the students also have modeling from the teacher and previous student collaborations to draw from.

If a student is working alone on a primary source analysis as part of an extension to his or her own learning, there should still be opportunities to check in. The student may check in with a partner more regularly and then with the teacher once or twice depending on how much of the work the student is doing independently. A teacher may do a quick check-in during the searching process if the student is looking for his or her own sources. Another check-in toward the end of the analysis to see the student's thoughts and next steps may also be helpful. These can be done in person or using an exit slip written about in Chapter 2.

A Final Hope and Setting Goals to Use Primary Source Analysis with Elementary Students

Hopefully this book has given you an idea of where the analysis of primary sources may play a part in your students' learning. Maybe there is an example that you use directly from the book. A curriculum connection may have come to you as you read. Possibly you have already gone on a search for primary sources from one of the places mentioned in the introduction. However the inspiration has happened, be sure to revisit the idea of every primary source analysis having a compelling source, specific analysis strategy, and connection to other learning.

As you look back after implementing your first primary source analysis, reflect on the roles you play and how your students react to those roles. What were the bright spots? Where did your students surprise you? How did your planning and implementing of the analysis support that success? What could have gone better? When could you have changed something you did to help make that happen? Use those reflections as goals when planning the next primary source analysis.

Like all learning, internalizing the skill of analyzing primary sources is most effective when revisited throughout the year. Think about how to build on the momentum of students' experiences in analyzing primary sources. Introducing a skill and practicing it again within days or weeks will reap more benefits to your students and to you compared to waiting for months. Consider setting a goal of introducing and revisiting primary source analysis with students.

However and whenever you decide to use primary sources in the classroom, I hope you see engagement, insightful observations, powerful connections, and deep questions from your students.

Bibliography

American Association of School Librarians. (2018). *Natonal school library standards for learners, school librarians, and school libraries.* Chicago, IL: ALA Editions, an imprint of the American Library Association.

Lehman, C., & Roberts, K. (2014). *Falling in love with close reading: Lessons for analyzing texts—and life.* Portsmouth, NH: Heinemann.

Stanford History Education Group. *Reading Like a Historian.* Stanford, CA: Stanford University. Retrieved from https://sheg.stanford.edu/history-lessons

Teacher Resources: Library of Congress. *Teacher's guides and analysis tool.* Washington, DC: Library of Congress. Retrieved from http://www.loc.gov/teachers/usingprimarysources/guides.html

Visible Thinking: Project Zero. *Visible Thinking.* Cambridge, MA: Harvard Graduate School of Education. Retrieved from http://www.pz.harvard.edu/projects/visible-thinking

Bibliography

Primary Source References

Figure 2.1   Workmen Constructing the Statue of Liberty in Bartholdi's Parisian
             Warehouse Workshop
Source: Fernique, Albert, 1841?–1898, photographer. *Workmen constructing the Statue of Liberty in Bartholdi's Parisian warehouse workshop; first model; left hand; and quarter-size head-; Winter ?.* France, Paris, 1882 [or 1883]. Photograph. https://www.loc.gov/item/97502750/

Figure 2.2   November 7, 1922, *Public Ledger*
Source: *The public ledger.* (Maysville, Ky.), 07 Nov. 1922. *Chronicling America: Historic American Newspapers.* Lib. of Congress. https://chronicling america.loc.gov/lccn/sn85038022/1922-11-07/ed-1/seq-4

Figure 2.3   September 25, 1919, *Evening Public Ledger*
Source: *Evening public ledger.* (Philadelphia [Pa.]), 25 Sept. 1919. *Chronicling America: Historic American Newspapers.* Lib. of Congress. https://chronicling america.loc.gov/lccn/sn83045211/1919-09-25/ed-1/seq-12/

Figure 2.5   Seven-year-old Alex Reiber Topping
Source: Hine, Lewis Wickes, 1874–1940, photographer. *Seven-year-old Alex Reiber topping. He said, "I hooked me knee with the beet-knife, but I jest went on a-workin'." Location: Sterling [vicinity], Colorado / Photo by Hine, Oct 23/15.* Sterling, Colorado, 1915. Photograph. https://www.loc.gov/item/ncl2004004307/PP/

Figure 2.6   December 6, 1909, *New-York Tribune*
Source: *New-York tribune.* (New York [N.Y.]), 06 Dec. 1909. *Chronicling America: Historic American Newspapers*. Lib. of Congress. https://chroniclingamerica.loc.gov/lccn/sn83030214/1909-12-06/ed-1/seq-1/

Figure 2.7   *The Diary of a Shirtwaist Striker* by Theresa Serber Malkiel
Source: Malkiel, Theresa Serber. *The Diary of a Shirtwaist Striker: A Story of the Shirtwaist Makers' Strike in New York.* 2nd ed. New York: The Co-operative Press, 1910. https://babel.hathitrust.org/cgi/pt?id=mdp.39015073391321; view=1up;seq=31

Figure 3.2   School Children's Thanksgiving Games
Source: Bain News Service, publisher. *School children's Thanksgiving Games, 11/27/11.* 27 Nov. 1911 (date created or published later by Bain). Photograph. https://www.loc.gov/item/2014689985/

Figure 3.3   To Stuff a Turkey
Source: Simmons, Amelia, and American Imprint Collection. *American cookery, or, the art of dressing viands, fish, poultry, and vegetables: and the best modes of making pastes, puffs, pies, tarts, puddings, custards, and preserves: and all kinds of cakes, from the imperial plumb to plain cake, adapted to this country, and all grades of life.* Hartford: Printed by Hudson & Goodwin for the Author, 1796. PDF. https://www.loc.gov/item/96126967/. https://www.loc.gov/resource/rbc0001.2015amimp26967/?sp=20

Figure 3.4   Thanksgiving in Camp Sketched Thursday 28th 1861
Source: Waud, Alfred R., 1828–1891, artist. *Thanksgiving in camp sketched Thursday 28th.* United States, 1861. Photograph. https://www.loc.gov/resource/ppmsca.21210/

Figure 3.5   18th-Century Primer
Source: Thomas, Isaiah, 1749–1831, printer. *A little pretty pocket-book: intended for the instruction and amusement of little Master Tommy, and pretty Miss Polly: with two letters from Jack the giant-killer, as also a ball and pincushion, the use of which will infallibly make Tommy a good boy, and Polly a good girl: to which is added, A little song-book, being a new attempt to teach children the use of the English alphabet, by way of diversion.* Printed at Worcester, Massachusetts: by Isaiah Thomas, and sold, wholesale and retail, at his bookstore, 1787. PDF. https://www.loc.gov/item/22005880/

Figure 4.2   May 28, 1916, *Arizona Republic*
Source: *Arizona republican.* (Phoenix, Ariz.), 28 May 1916. *Chronicling America: Historic American Newspapers.* Lib. of Congress. https://chronicling america.loc.gov/lccn/sn84020558/1916-05-28/ed-1/seq-8/

Figure 4.3   April 6, 1916, Philadelphia *Evening Public Ledger*
Source: *Evening public ledger.* (Philadelphia [Pa.]), 06 April 1916. *Chronicling America: Historic American Newspapers.* Lib. of Congress. https://chronicling america.loc.gov/lccn/sn83045211/1916-04-06/ed-1/seq-9/

Figure 4.4   May 27, 1916, Klamath Falls *Evening Herald*
Source: *The evening herald.* (Klamath Falls, Or.), 27 May 1916. *Chronicling America: Historic American Newspapers.* Lib. of Congress. https://chronicling america.loc.gov/lccn/sn99063812/1916-05-27/ed-1/seq-4/

Figure 4.5   Miss Richardson and Mrs. A. S. Burke
Source: Miss Richardson and Mrs. A. S. Burke. Bain News Service, publisher. (Source: Flickr Commons project, 2014). LC-DIG-ggbain-21396. https://www.loc.gov/pictures/item/2014701334/

Figure 4.6   Golden Flyer Leaving N.Y. 4/6/16
Source: "Golden Flyer" leaving N.Y., 4/6/16. Bain News Service, publisher. LC-DIG-ggbain-21391. https://www.loc.gov/item/2014701329/

Figure 4.7   April 23, 1916, *New-York Tribune*
Source: *New-York tribune.* (New York [N.Y.]), 23 April 1916. *Chronicling America: Historic American Newspapers.* Lib. of Congress. https://chroniclingamerica.loc.gov/lccn/sn83030214/1916-04-23/ed-1/seq-8/

Figure 4.8   April 17, 1916, *New-York Tribune*
Source: *New-York tribune.* (New York [N.Y.]), 17 April 1916. *Chronicling America: Historic American Newspapers.* Lib. of Congress. https://chronicling america.loc.gov/lccn/sn83030214/1916-04-17/ed-1/seq-9/

Figure 4.9   May 2, 1916, *New-York Tribune*.
Source: New-*York tribune.* (New York [N.Y.]), 02 May 1916. *Chronicling America: Historic American Newspapers.* Lib. of Congress. https://chroniclingamerica.loc.gov/lccn/sn83030214/1916-05-02/ed-1/seq-8/

Figure 5.1   Thanksgiving
Source: Bain News Service, publisher. *Thanksgiving*, [between ca. 1910 and c. 1915]. Photograph. https://www.loc.gov/item/2014694901/

Figure 5.2   April 17, 1878, *Forest Republican*
Source: *The Forest Republican*. (Tionesta, Pa.), 17 April 1878. *Chronicling America: Historic American Newspapers*. Lib. of Congress. https://chronicling america.loc.gov/lccn/sn84026497/1878-04-17/ed-1/seq-4/

Figure 5.3   Colossal Hand and Torch "Liberty"
Source: Philadelphia: Centennial Photographic Co., c. 1876. Library of Congress Prints and Photographs Division. LC-DIG-ppmsca-02957. https://www.loc.gov/pictures/item/97502738/

Figure 5.4   Workmen Constructing the Statue of Liberty in Bartholdi's Parisian Warehouse Workshop
Source: Fernique, Albert, 1841?–1898, photographer. *Workmen constructing the Statue of Liberty in Bartholdi's Parisian warehouse workshop; first model; left hand; and quarter-size head-; Winter ?*. France, Paris, 1882 [or 1883]. Photograph. https://www.loc.gov/item/97502750/

Figure 5.5   November 24, 1913, *New-York Tribune*
Source: *New-York tribune*. (New York [N.Y.]), 24 Nov. 1913. *Chronicling America: Historic American Newspapers*. Lib. of Congress. https://chronicling america.loc.gov/lccn/sn83030214/1913-11-24/ed-1/seq-6/

Figure 5.6   First Flight, 120 Feet in 12 Seconds 10:35 a.m.; Kitty Hawk, North Carolina
Source: Wright, Wilbur, 1867–1912, Orville Wright, 1871–1948, and John T. Daniels, 1873–1948, photographer. *First flight, 120 feet in 12 seconds, 10:35 a.m.; Kitty Hawk, North Carolina*, 1903. Photograph. https://www.loc.gov/item/00652085/

Figure 5.7   December 17th Diary Entry of Orville Wright
Source: [Diary, Orville Wright, 1903]. Diaries and Notebooks: 1903, Orville Wright. Wilbur and Orville Wright Papers, Manuscript Division, Library of Congress. https://www.loc.gov/resource/mwright.01007/?sp=28

Figure 5.8   June 14, 1916, *Carson City Daily Appeal*
Source: *Carson City daily appeal*. (Carson City, Nev.), 14 June 1916. *Chronicling America: Historic American Newspapers*. Lib. of Congress. https://chronicling america.loc.gov/lccn/sn86076241/1916-06-14/ed-1/seq-1/

Index

Addams, Jane, 124
American Association of School Librarians (AASL), 3–4
American Civil War, 84
Analyzing Like a Historian strategy, 57–71; differentiating, for youngest learners, 70; framing, 57–59; guiding students through, 59–66; overview, 57; teacher's role in, 66–69
Arizona Republic, 117
Around America to Win the Vote (Rockliff), 121
Audiovisual primary source. *See* Primary source sounds and moving pictures

Bibliographic data, 60
Boston Massacre, 7
Brave Girl, 59
Burke, Alice, 117, 121, 126, 129, 131, 155

Career, and Civic Life (C3) Framework, 3
Carson City Daily Appeal, 156
Cartoons, 85
Chronicling America, 8
Close Reading strategy, 30–43; developing understanding, 37–39; differentiating, for youngest learners, 42–43; finding patterns in reading, 35–37; framing, 31–33; guiding students through, 33–39; lens of word choice, 33–35; overview, 31; teacher's role in, 39–42
Collaboration: configurations during primary source analysis, 134–37; pair, 135–36; and

primary source analysis, 136–37; small-group, 134–35; as a way to address student misconceptions, 137–39; whole-class, 134
Compelling primary sources, 80–84; characteristics, 81–84; connections, 81; emotional reaction, 82–84; familiarity, 81; format, 82
Connections, and compelling primary sources, 81
Contextualization, 62–63
Corroboration, 65–66

Dangerous Jane (Slade), 124
The Diary of a Shirtwaist Striker: A Story of the Shirtwaist Makers' Strike in New York (Malkiel), 61
Digital Public Library of America (DPLA), 8
Digital viewing, of text-based primary sources, 103
DOCSTeach, 8
Documenting: primary source audio analysis, 110–12; primary source video and film analysis, 112
Drawings, 85–86

Edison Studios, 106
Emotional reaction, and compelling primary sources, 82–84
Emotions, and audiovisual primary source, 107–9
Engravings, 85–86

Equipment, and audiovisual primary source, 109
Evening Herald, 119
Evening Public Ledger, 118
Exit slips, 73–76

Falling in Love with Close Reading (Lehman and Roberts), 30
Familiarity, and compelling primary sources, 81
Fernique, Albert, 144
Forest Republican, 141
Format, and compelling primary sources, 82
Foundational literacy, 2

Graphic organizers, 69

Handwriting, in primary source text, 97–99
Harvard, 71, 104
Hine, Lewis, 43, 124

Images, in primary source text, 101. *See also* Drawings
Independent instruction, and primary sources, 141–43

Jigsaw strategy, 103–4
Jump In strategy, 92–93

Language arts: and primary sources, 121–28; and visual literacy, 123–24
Lehman, Christopher, 30
Lens of word choice, 33–35
Library of Congress, 7–8, 30, 43, 106
Lincoln, Abraham, 60–61
Listening, during a primary source analysis, 145–48
Literacy: foundational, 2; media, 2; visual, 2, 123
Long passages, of primary source text, 100
Long S, in primary source texts, 99

Malkiel, Theresa Serber, 61
Maths, and primary sources, 130–32
Media literacy, 2
Modeling, in primary source analysis, 28

National Child Labor Committee Collection, 43
National Council for the Social Studies (NCSS) College, 3
National School Library Standards, 3

New-York Tribune, 126, 129, 131
Next Generation Science Standards, 3

Observations, in See, Wonder, Think strategy, 47–48

Pair collaboration, 135–36
Pairing primary sources, 151–57; to answer questions, 152–54; to extend or broaden a topic, 155–57; with multiple perspectives, 151–52; need for, 151; to reinforce understandings and ideas, 154–55
Photo primary sources, 151
Political cartoons, 85. *See also* Cartoons
Portraits, 85–86
Pose strategy, 93–95
Primary source analysis: as assessment, 143–45; and collaboration, 136–37; collaboration configurations during, 134–37; listening during, 145–48; responding during, 148–51; student misconceptions and collaboration, 137–39; teachers use of, 139–45
Primary-source-analysis strategy: students collaboration, 16–17; students' role, 15–16; teachers' role, 14–15; Visible Thinking strategies, 71–78. *See also* Primary sources; *specific strategies*
Primary Source Analysis Tool, 30
Primary source images: analyzing, 85–95; considerations in selecting, 85–86; modified analysis for, 89–95; student interactions with, 87–95; text in, 86; types of, 85
Primary sources: analyzing, 2–5; compelling, 80–84; described, 5–7; and elementary students, 157–58; identifying, 7–9; movement within, 107; pairing, 151–57; preparing to use, 9–11; and subject area, 114–32. –*See also* Primary-source-analysis strategy
Primary source sounds and moving pictures: analyzing, 105–12; considerations when selecting, 106–9; student interactions with, 109–12; types of, 105–6
Primary source text: analyzing, 95–105; considerations when selecting, 96–101; handwriting in, 97–99; images in, 101; long passages of, 100; long S in, 99; student interactions with, 101–5; transcripts of, 103; types of, 95–96; vocabulary in, 96–97
Project Zero, 71, 104
Puzzle strategy, 90–92

Ratterree, Alice, 124
Reading Like a Historian strategy, 57
Responding, during primary source analysis, 148–51
Revere, Paul, 7
Richardson, Nell, 117, 121, 155
Riis, Jacob, 124
Roberts, Kate, 30
Rockliff, Mara, 126

School Children's Thanksgiving Games, 11/27/11, 82, 83
School families, 8–9
Science, and primary sources, 128–30
See, Think, Wonder strategy, 17–30; differentiating for youngest learners, 29–30; framing, 18–20; guiding students through, 20–24; overview, 17–18; teacher's role in, 25–29
See, Wonder, Think strategy, 43–57; differentiating, for youngest learners, 56–57; framing, 43–46; guiding students through, 46–53; overview, 43; teacher's role in, 53–56
Shirtwaist makers' strike, 58–59, 61–62, 75
Sketches, 85–86
Slade, Suzanne, 124
Small-group collaboration, 134–35
Smith, Trey, 115
Smithsonian Learning Lab, 8
Social studies: and *Arizona Republic* article, 117; different disciplines within, 117–21; and primary sources, 116–21
Sound, and audiovisual primary source, 106–7
Sourcing, 60–62
Stanford History Education Group, 57
"The Statue for New York Harbor," 141
Statue of Liberty, 6, 18–20
Student(s): and Analyzing Like a Historian strategy, 59–66; and Close Reading strategy, 33–39; collaborating through primary source analysis, 16–17; misconceptions and collaboration, 137–39; and primary source images, 87–95; primary source sounds and moving pictures, 109–12; and primary source text, 101–5; role in primary source analysis, 15–16; and See, Think, Wonder strategy, 20–24; and See, Wonder, Think

strategy, 46–53; and Visible Thinking strategies, 72–73
Subject area: language arts, 121–28; maths, 130–32; and primary sources, 114–32; science, 128–30; social studies, 116–21

Teacher(s): and Analyzing Like a Historian strategy, 66–69; and Close Reading strategy, 39–42; as documenter of student thinking, 25; role as facilitator, 25, 54; role in framing primary source analysis, 14–15; and See, Think, Wonder strategy, 25–29; and See, Wonder, Think strategy, 53–56; and Visible Thinking strategies, 76–78
Thanksgiving celebration, 84
Thanksgiving in Camp Sketched Thursday 28th 1861, 84
Time, and audiovisual primary source, 106
TPS Teachers Network, 8
Transcripts, of primary source text, 103

Verbalization, 41
Visible Thinking strategies, 71–78; differentiating, for youngest learners, 78; exit slips examples, 73–76; framing, 72; guiding students through, 72–73; overview, 71–72; teacher's role in, 76–78
Visual literacy, 2, 123
Vocabulary, in primary source text, 96–97

Washington, George, 6
Whole-class collaboration, 134
Whole-class instruction, and primary sources, 140–41
Workmen constructing the Statue of Liberty in Bartholdi's Parisian warehouse workshop; first model; left hand; and quarter-size head-; Winter 1882?, 18–19
Wright, Orville, 154
Wright brothers', 153

Youngest learners: and Analyzing Like a Historian strategy, 70; and Close Reading strategy, 42–43; and See, Think, Wonder strategy, 29–30; and See, Wonder, Think strategy, 56–57; and use of image- or video-based primary sources, 29; and Visible Thinking strategies, 78

About the Author

TOM BOBER is an elementary librarian in Clayton, Missouri, former Teacher in Residence at the Library of Congress, a 2018 Library Journal Mover and Shaker, and member of the Teacher and Educator Advisory Board at the National Portrait Gallery and American Archive of Public Broadcasting. He has written about the uses and benefits of primary sources in classrooms for *School Library Connection*, *Social Education* magazine, *Library of Congress Magazine*, *American Libraries*, and *School Library Journal*. Tom also writes the Pairing Picture Books and Primary Sources posts for the American Association of School Librarians *KQ* blog. He presents at regional and national conferences, runs workshops, and has developed and presented webinars for the Library of Congress and ABC-CLIO.

CPSIA information can be obtained
at www.ICGtesting.com
Printed in the USA
FSHW021846100520
70102FS